Parenting Isn't Personal

Reclaiming Your Identity and Joy in the Journey of Parenthood

Tanya Orr

© **Copyright 2024 - All rights reserved.**

The content contained within this book may not be reproduced, duplicated or transmitted without direct written permission from the author or the publisher.

Under no circumstances will any blame or legal responsibility be held against the publisher, or author, for any damages, reparation, or monetary loss due to the information contained within this book, either directly or indirectly.

Legal Notice:

This book is copyright protected. It is only for personal use. You cannot amend, distribute, sell, use, quote or paraphrase any part, or the content within this book, without the consent of the author or publisher.

Disclaimer Notice:

Please note the information contained within this document is for educational and entertainment purposes only. All effort has been executed to present accurate, up to date, reliable, complete information. No warranties of any kind are declared or implied. Readers acknowledge that the author is not engaged in the rendering of legal, financial, medical or professional advice. The content within this book has been derived from various sources. Please consult a licensed professional before attempting any techniques outlined in this book.

By reading this document, the reader agrees that under no circumstances is the author responsible for any losses, direct or indirect, that are incurred as a result of the use of the information contained within this document, including, but not limited to, errors, omissions, or inaccuracies.

Table of Contents

INTRODUCTION: OUR FAMILY IS JUST THE RIGHT MIX OF CHAOS AND LOVE 1

- A Message to My Younger Self 2
- The Turning Point 3
- What This Book Will Teach You 4
- Moving Forward 5

CHAPTER 1: BREAKING FREE FROM THE PERFECT PARENT TRAP 7

- The Perfection Pressure Cooker 7
  - *What Society Tells First-Time Parents* 9
  - *What Society Tells Seasoned Parents* 11
- Social Media and Parenting Expectations 15
  - *Create a Family Media Plan* 17
  - *Lead by Example* 17
  - *Engage in Offline Activities* 17
- Embracing Imperfection—Your Path to Freedom 18
  - *Redefining "Good Parenting"* 18
  - *Learning From Mistakes* 19
  - *Finding Joy in the Journey* 20

CHAPTER 2: UNLOCKING THE MYSTERY OF YOUR CHILD'S BEHAVIOR 23

- Your Child Is Not Your Mirror 23
- The Mini-Me Myth 25
  - *Understanding Individuality* 25
  - *Separating Identity From Behavior* 27
  - *Managing Expectations Through Objective Parenting* 29
- What's *REALLY* Going On? Decoding Their Behavior 30
  - *The Basics of Child Development* 31
  - *Emotional Triggers* 32
  - *Communication Beyond Words* 34
  - *Empathy in Action* 35

CHAPTER 3: YOU AND YOUR EMOTIONS MATTER TOO 37

- Permission to Feel: Why Your Emotions Are Valid 37
  - *The Myth of the Selfless Parent* 38
  - *The Power of Acknowledgement* 40
  - *Emotional Intelligence for Parents* 41
- Communicating Needs Within the Family 44

- *The Art of Constructive Expression* *44*
- *Emotional Honesty With Children* *46*
- CONFLICT RESOLUTION AND EMOTIONAL REPAIR 47
  - *D—Describe* *47*
  - *E—Express* *47*
  - *S—Specify* *48*
  - *O—Outcome* *48*

CHAPTER 4: LIVING YOUR DREAM WHILE RAISING A FAMILY 49

- KEEPING YOUR FIRE ALIVE 49
  - *Identifying Your Passions* *51*
- BALANCING DREAMS AND DUTIES 53
  - *Time Management Basics for Busy Parents* *54*
  - *Bonding With Your Family Over Shared Passions* *57*

CHAPTER 5: KNOWING WHEN TO HIT THE PAUSE BUTTON 59

- THE WARNING SIGNS OF BEING OVERWHELMED 59
  - *Early Signs to Recognize* *61*
- CREATING YOUR OWN SPACE: CARVING OUT TIME IN A BUSY LIFE 62
  - *Give Yourself Pep Talks* *63*
  - *Communicate Your Need for Alone Time* *64*
  - *Design a Personal Sanctuary* *64*
  - *Set Boundaries* *65*
- QUIZ TIME: HOW WELL ARE YOU PRACTICING SELF-CARE? 66

CHAPTER 6: ASKING FOR HELP IS A STRENGTH, NOT A WEAKNESS 69

- REDEFINING STRENGTH 69
- HOW TO MASTER DELEGATION 71
  - *Start Small* *72*
  - *Choose the Right Individual for Each Task* *72*
  - *Communicate Instructions Clearly* *72*
  - *Offer Constructive Feedback* *73*
- FINDING THE RIGHT HELP, PROFESSIONAL OR PERSONAL 74
  - *Find Your Tribe* *75*
  - *How to Ask for Support* *76*

CHAPTER 7: REDEFINING WHAT SUCCESS MEANS IN PARENTING 79

- EMBRACING THE GROWTH MINDSET 79
  - *Find Purpose in Failure* *81*
  - *Allow Your Children to Dream* *81*
  - *Focus on Principles, Not Perfection* *82*
  - *Provide Growth-Oriented Feedback* *83*
- AFFIRM YOUR PARENTING REALITY 85
  - *Don't Deny How You Feel* *85*

See Things As They Are, Not As You Wish Them to Be 86
Validate Your Fears 86
Normalize Not Being Happy All the Time 87
CELEBRATE THE SMALL WINS: FIND JOY IN THE EVERYDAY 87

CHAPTER 8: THE RIPPLE EFFECT: LONG-TERM BENEFITS OF PRIORITIZING YOURSELF 91

THE CONNECTION BETWEEN SELF-CARE AND RESILIENCE 92
Encouraging Independence Through Self-Care 93
Offer Choices 94
Encourage Healthy Risk-Taking 94
Lead From Behind 94
Pick Your Battles 95
CREATING A HEALTHY FAMILY DYNAMIC 95
CELEBRATING THE RIPPLE EFFECT 97
Be Available for Yourself 97
Listen, But Don't Be Quick to Fix 97
Stand Up for Yourself 98
Don't Be a Buzz Kill 98
Express Gratitude 98

CONCLUSION: EMBRACING THE JOURNEY AHEAD WITH GRACE 101

BONUS CONTENT: ADDITIONAL RESOURCES 103

MUST READ BOOKS: PARENTING AND PERSONAL GROWTH 104
The Whole-Brain Child 104
How to Stop Losing Your Sh*t with Your Kids 104
Raising Good Humans 104
Daring Greatly 105
Parenting from the Inside Out 105
PROFESSIONAL AND PEER SUPPORT SERVICES 105
BetterHelp 106
Talkspace 106
Postpartum Support International (PSI) 106
Mothers of Preschoolers (MOPS) 106
La Leche League International 107
Parents Helping Parents (PHP) 107
The Village 107
SELF-SOOTHING STRESS MANAGEMENT PRACTICES 107
Mindful Breathing 108
Gratitude Journaling 108
Stretching Routine 109
Morning Meditation 110
Setting Daily Intentions 110

Nature Walks *111*
Positive Affirmations *111*
Digital Detox *112*
Scheduled Family Moments *113*

REFERENCES 115
IMAGE REFERENCES 123

Introduction: Our Family is Just the Right Mix of Chaos and Love

Our family is just the right mix of chaos and love. –Anonymous

Parenthood is a beautiful, messy, and sometimes overwhelming journey that is different for everyone. As a mother of nine children, ages ranging from 4 to 21, both biological and adoptive, my parenting journey has been filled with every possible emotion. Each of my children has their own distinct personality—some easier than others—all with unique strengths, challenges, likes, and dislikes. They are all mine, and like any mother, I only want the best for them: to reach their greatest potential and be healthy, safe, and confident in who they are. I want them to believe in themselves, to be smart and emotionally stable, and to trust their instincts.

But with all those hopes comes the endless worry that keeps us up at night. We buy books, talk to friends, seek advice from experts, and, when desperation sets in at 2 a.m., we turn to Google, searching for answers we've already asked about countless times. As parents, we all yearn for reassurance that our feelings are valid. We want someone to tell us, "You're right for feeling that way. Don't worry, you're not crazy; you're just a parent."

Raising nine children has taught me more than any parenting book ever could. It's a journey filled with highs and lows, triumphs and tears, joy and frustration. And despite all the advice, strategies, and guidance I've sought over the years, there were moments when I felt that something was missing—a validation of my own needs and emotions. Too often, parenting resources focus solely on what the parent should do differently: how to improve, how to change, and how to adapt. Yes, those strategies are valuable, but what about acknowledging that parenting is hard and that it's okay to feel overwhelmed, frustrated, and even lost sometimes?

A Message to My Younger Self

If I could go back and give advice to my younger self before this wild ride of motherhood began, I would start by saying, "Buckle up—this is going to be the hardest thing you'll ever do." Loving someone so deeply means that when they ache, you ache; when they hunger, you forget to eat; and while they sleep, you pray. You give everything—your time, energy, and sometimes even your last bit of patience—without expecting anything in return. And yet, there will be days when it feels like all your efforts go unnoticed. Your children may forget to say thank you, they may roll their eyes when you set boundaries, and sometimes, even though you give your all, it still won't feel like enough.

I would tell my younger self that it's okay to take a step back and that perfection is an illusion. Despite your best intentions, you won't always get it right—and that's okay. Your children aren't perfect either, so give yourself some grace. Don't forget to love yourself as fiercely as you love them. It's okay if they roll their eyes when you say no, and it's okay to remind them that you were once a kid too—you know how to roll your eyes just as well as they do!

I would remind myself that being a parent doesn't mean sacrificing every part of who you are. It's okay to pursue your own dreams, have boundaries, and prioritize your needs alongside your children's. You don't have to put your life on hold for 18 years. Your identity matters, and nurturing yourself doesn't take away from your ability to be a loving, committed parent.

The Turning Point

For years, I had thought about writing this book, but it wasn't until one Mother's Day that the turning point came. I watched as a mother went viral for sharing her raw, unfiltered feelings with the world. She sat teary-eyed in front of the camera explaining how not one of her six children had acknowledged her on Mother's Day. She talked about all she had sacrificed—her education, career, and countless personal dreams—all to be there for them. I felt every word she said, and it struck a chord deep within me.

I wanted to reach through the screen and tell her, and every other mother out there, "Don't give up on yourself. You deserve to pursue your dreams, too. Life is too short to put yourself on hold, waiting for your children to validate your sacrifices. There is a way to have it all—yourself and them. You can be the best parent while also being the best version of yourself."

This book isn't about being selfish; it's about leading by example. It's about showing your children what it means to live a balanced, whole, and fulfilling life. It's about being everything you want them to be: dreamers, go-getters, lifelong learners, and compassionate individuals who prioritize their well-being. It's about embracing the messiness of parenthood while also embracing your own needs, desires, and aspirations.

What This Book Will Teach You

Throughout this book, you'll find practical guidance and encouragement to help you redefine what it means to be a successful parent. Here's a glimpse of what you can expect:

Breaking Free From the Perfect Parent Trap: You'll learn to let go of unrealistic expectations and embrace the freedom that comes with imperfection.

Unlocking the Mystery of Your Child's Behavior: We'll explore how to understand your child's actions without taking them personally and how to support them as unique individuals.

You and Your Emotions Matter Too: Discover the importance of acknowledging your own feelings and communicating your needs within your family.

Living Your Dream While Raising a Family: Find out how to pursue your passions and integrate them into your life, even amidst the chaos of parenting.

Knowing When to Hit the Pause Button: Learn strategies for recognizing overwhelm and creating space for yourself to recharge and reset.

Asking for Help Is a Strength, Not a Weakness: We'll discuss the importance of building a support system and seeking help without guilt.

Redefining What Success Means in Parenting: You'll be encouraged to create your own definition of success, one that aligns with your values and brings joy to your journey.

The Ripple Effect—Long-Term Benefits of Prioritizing Yourself: Discover how your self-care not only benefits you but also sets a powerful example for your children and future generations.

Embracing the Journey Ahead with Grace: In the conclusion, we'll reflect on the lessons learned and inspire you to move forward with confidence, compassion, and an open heart.

Moving Forward

This book is a call to action for every parent who has ever felt overwhelmed, undervalued, or uncertain. It's a reminder that you are allowed to be both a masterpiece and a work in progress and that your journey as a parent is uniquely yours. You matter. Your dreams matter. And by embracing your needs alongside those of your children, you create a life rich in love, balance, and fulfillment.

As you read through the pages of this book, I hope you find the validation, encouragement, and practical guidance you need to navigate your parenting journey with renewed strength and a sense of purpose. Together, let's embrace the beautiful chaos of parenthood and remember that you can be both the best parent and the best version of yourself.

Chapter 1:

Breaking Free from the Perfect Parent Trap

There is no such thing as a perfect parent. So just be a real one. –Sue Atkins

The Perfection Pressure Cooker

One of the handy kitchen gadgets I have used on countless occasions to prepare delicious meals for my family is the pressure cooker. Unlike conventional cooking methods, where a pot sits on a gas or electric stovetop and gradually heats the food until cooked through, the pressure cooker uses hot spluttering steam trapped inside the pot to increase the boiling point and cook the food at a higher temperature. The result is tender, flavorful meals prepared in a fraction of the time.

Many parents, especially mothers, are trapped inside a "perfection pressure cooker." Imagine that the expectations of parenthood were a metaphoric pot that some first-time and seasoned parents feel trapped inside. The more they seek to live up to these expectations, the more pressure they experience. Eventually, each parent inside the pot reaches their "boiling point"—the maximum threshold of stress and anxiety they can bear before breaking down—and can either let go of these expectations or collapse under the heavy burden of them.

There is much talk about good versus bad parenting and what parents should and shouldn't do to give their children the best start in life. These conversations, which are sometimes started by experts, cause many parents to feel an immense amount of pressure to live up to high expectations. At the end of the day, no parent desires to fail at raising their children, so advice from different sources is always welcomed. What's confusing, however, is that many times this advice is contradictory, creating ambiguous and unrealistic standards. For example, how many times have you heard the following sentiments from parenting articles, books, or podcasts:

- "Be firm with your child but not too strict."
- "Show your child affection, but don't coddle them."
- "Don't shelter your child, but protect them from the many dangers of this world."
- "Follow your instincts, but consult a doctor when you notice any worrying signs."
- "Give your child privacy, but stay informed about their lives at all times."
- "Teach your child to set boundaries, but ensure they are polite and respectful."

You may not have questioned this advice when you first heard it because it came from a credible source like your close friend, doctor, or a parenting group you respect. However, as you process this advice, you become less sure of the right approach to parenting your child. All that you do know is that you aren't doing enough to raise your child the "perfect way."

What Society Tells First-Time Parents

Bringing a child into the world is a magical and unforgettable experience, especially when it's your first time being a parent. Nevertheless, society tends to paint an unrealistic picture of what parenthood should look or feel like during those early weeks and months. Without realizing it, you may feel pressure to follow specific parenting models or make sure your child meets milestones that you are told are the bare minimum at their life stage. When you don't live up to these high expectations, you might internalize that as a personal failure, which isn't true or fair. Here are some common pressures that first-time parents experience and ways that you can navigate them.

Full Post-Partum Recovery Should Take a Few Months

As a first-time parent, you wonder when your life will go back to normal after bringing your child into the world. Some of the things you might miss about your old life include your body and fitness level, feeling mentally and emotionally stable, following a consistent routine, and spending time with your partner or alone. Many online sources will tell you it only takes a few months to return to your normal self. If you are active on social media, you might even see before and after photos of women who lost pregnancy weight within weeks of giving birth. But how realistic are these expectations?

Every woman's pregnancy journey won't look the same. This isn't because some women are more prepared for pregnancy than others but instead a result of a combination of factors, such as pregnancy complications, one versus multiple pregnancies, genetics, medical history, mental health, lifestyle, and environment. Post-partum recovery involves more than going on a diet and planning date nights with your partner; your resilient mind and body need time to heal from the physical, mental, and emotional changes that occurred over the past nine months. For some women, this can take three months; for others, it might take three years, or they may never reach the point of complete recovery.

Being compassionate toward yourself post-delivery can help you manage your stress levels and undergo recovery at your body's pace and time. Dr. Kristin Neff, a pioneering researcher on the subject of self-compassion, describes the emotion as treating yourself like you would a friend (Neff, 2024). In moments when you are tempted to compare your post-partum journey with other mothers or families, ask yourself: Would I encourage my friend to make comparisons? Whenever your inner critic wakes up on the wrong side of the bed and demands to see progress in your health, routine, and social life, ask yourself: Would I impose such rigid standards on my friend?

Well-Raised Children Won't Be Fussy or Difficult

There's this prevailing idea among parenting circles that newborns and toddlers shouldn't be fussy or difficult, otherwise the parents must be doing something wrong. Behaviors like crying, whining, or refusing to eat and sleep are seen as troublesome and need to be corrected through strict schedules and discipline. What's often forgotten is that newborns and toddlers don't have refined speaking skills like we do and, therefore, use non-verbal behaviors like crying, whining, or refusing to eat and sleep to communicate their discomfort or distress to us. They are also in the process of learning how to be socialized and why some behaviors—like throwing tantrums—are less desirable than others.

The next time your child is called fussy or difficult by good-intentioned friends or family, tell them that they are simply being a child. They didn't come into this world with the intellect of Einstein, so they need to learn social and emotional skills through exploration and experimentation. If you sometimes find yourself feeling annoyed or embarrassed with your child for not showing the same behaviors as other children, remind yourself that they are an individual who will grow up with a unique personality, mindset, and mannerisms. They are not supposed to be like other children; they simply need to feel safe discovering who they are.

It's okay to raise a child who requires more instruction, attention, and support to behave properly. Their needs may be different, but they aren't an inconvenience. Similar to how you have unexplained mood swings, emotional triggers, or irrational fears, your child's emotional life is just as complex. The only difference is they may not be as skilled at regulating their emotions.

Good Parents Place Their Children's Needs Above Their Own

How many times have you heard this phrase: "If you love your child, you will do anything for them?" Maybe you have said it to someone or thought about it several times in the past. While it comes across as an expression of unconditional love, the reality is that it's a sign of unchecked boundaries. Unconditional love is a sacrificial type of love that seeks the best for your child and loved ones but not at the expense of your dignity and well-being (Brady-Cronin, 2023).

As much as you are ready and willing to respond to your child's every cry, call, and request, there will be times when taking care of your needs will come first. Prepare for times when you can hear your child crying but need to quickly fold the few pieces of laundry so you can check that task off your to-do list. Be ready sometimes to distract your children with arts and crafts activities while you go into the other room and enjoy a cup of coffee or finish the episode you had left on pause for the last hour. Instead of seeing your needs as limitations that stop you from pouring all the love you have into your child, choose to see them as regulators that ensure that whatever you are pouring into your child comes from a surplus rather than a deficit of what you have inside.

Think of the instructions you receive before the plane takes off, which is to place an oxygen mask over yourself before assisting other passengers. Was that instruction designed to be a limitation or regulator? Does it hinder or promote your safety? The same can be said about keeping a good sleep schedule, eating meals regularly throughout the day, and finding five minutes now and again to breathe and introspect. These healthy forms of self-care are regulators that allow you to continue loving and nurturing your child without feeling overstretched.

What Society Tells Seasoned Parents

Seasoned parents don't have it easier just because they aren't new to parenting; they, too, feel the pressure to raise their children a certain way.

For instance, there are unspoken social codes and norms you are expected to teach and enforce in your children to make them feel accepted by your community. When your children embody these codes and norms, it not only makes them appear successful according to society but also makes you look good to others and receive comments like "Oh, what a smart and responsible young man you have raised" or "Your daughter is such a pleasure to teach!" The cost of being externally validated by society is restricting your children from authentically displaying who they are and holding yourself up to standards that are too high. Here are some of the common pressures that seasoned parents will face and how to navigate them.

You Should Have Parenting Figured Out

After the first child, society is less tolerant and forgiving of parents asking for help, expressing grievances, making mistakes, or generally having bad days. You are expected to have achieved balance, created systems, and understood how to respond to each child's needs. The fear of failure or humiliation can sometimes cause you to put up a tough exterior when, deep down, you desire to have someone who can listen to your challenges and offer guidance.

As a mother of nine, I can tell you from my firsthand experience that you never fully figured out parenting. The moment you think you've cracked the Rubix cube, a new variable pops up and leaves you with more questions than answers. Additionally, every child is different and may not handle each life stage the same way as their older or younger sibling. For example, your three children could have three unique puberty experiences, which require you to have three completely different parenting approaches to connect with them.

The trick is to maintain a beginner's mindset, no matter how many years of parenting experience you have. This type of mindset allows you to see hidden lessons behind every parenting situation and gain more wisdom. Instead of pretending that you have it all figured out, be willing to admit that you don't without feeling ashamed. Expressing this level of vulnerability is uncomfortable at first but liberating when you discover that you aren't the only seasoned parent who still has breakdowns and isn't always confident in their decisions. The beginner's mindset encourages you to seek support, ask questions, and bounce back from every setback, stronger than you were before.

Your Older Children Should Make You Proud

Seasoned parents are sometimes judged for the way their children turn out. For instance, you might feel pressure to make sure your children succeed at school, head off to college, find stable employment, and stand on their own. If you have a child with a developmental disorder or any other form of mental health or behavioral condition, you might feel the need to prove to others that they can achieve favorable life outcomes like other children. But in retrospect, who needs to feel proud of the way your children turn out? Is it you, your friends and family, or your children?

Your duty as a present and loving parent is to raise your children the best way you know how so they can get a good start in life. But with that said, cultivating a safe and nurturing environment at home doesn't guarantee that your children will follow in your footsteps or take the conventional route that other children have chosen. It's important for them to feel proud and secure in the life paths they have decided to take, even if that means going against their family's traditions or society's expectations.

In addition to this, remind yourself often that you are not responsible for your children's actions, whether good or bad, since that is something you cannot control. Perhaps you can tell a five-year-old what to do, and they will listen to you but don't expect to get that same feedback from your fifteen-year-old. It's not that your older child is disrespectful; they have simply gone through the process of individuation and have constructed a separate identity from you. Practice respecting your children's decisions while simultaneously managing your expectations of them. You don't need to always approve of what they do, particularly as they get older and become young adults, but you can recognize their right to make choices concerning their lives.

You Should Have the Perfect Marriage or Co-parenting Relationship

Society often expects seasoned parents to achieve the perfect balance between their spousal or co-parenting relationships and parenting. For example, women might feel the pressure to be exceptional wives and mothers; men might feel the pressure to be awesome husbands and fathers. In reality, these roles have separate requirements and standards. The trouble is that many seasoned parents become so fixated on their parenting roles that they fail to learn what is expected of them in their partnerships. Some might even use parenting techniques to nurture your marriage or co-parenting relationship. However, you cannot use a cookie recipe to bake a cake and expect it to come out perfectly.

Perfect marriages or co-parenting relationships don't exist. The closest you can get to one is showing commitment to growing with your partner and navigating each phase of your relationship as a team. Outside of caring for your children, you can find other things to bond over, such as your shared interests, hobbies, or goals. Not only does this allow you to have a more well-rounded and fulfilling relationship, but you also have topics to divert to when you want to relieve tension and stress.

It is also important to accept that not all parents get married or stay married, and not all co-parenting relationships will be amicable. Nevertheless, it's possible to still provide your children with a healthy and happy home life even when you don't have the support of a significant other. Ideally, every child would be raised in a home with two parents, but when that can't happen, don't beat yourself up about it. Later in life, when your children recall their childhoods, they won't remember the life you couldn't give them. Instead, they will think back to moments when you showed up, offered encouragement, and supported them the best way you could.

The "perfect parent" mindset, which burdens both first-time and seasoned parents, is not a modern phenomenon. It can be traced back to social, cultural, and gender norms, extending as far as prehistoric times. Early humans, living in the wild, relied on survival instincts and communal support to keep themselves and their children alive. For them, being a "perfect" parent meant something similar to what it means for us today—caring for their children as if their very survival depended on it. However, to challenge this deeply ingrained mindset and quiet the survival instinct that still drives many parents, we should ask ourselves: Does our survival *still* depend on our parenting abilities today?

Social Media and Parenting Expectations

We can't speak about the "perfection pressure cooker" without discussing the role of social media. When parents jumped on the social media train in the early 2000s, few anticipated how this positive communication tool could become potentially harmful, not only for their mental and emotional well-being but also for how they raise their children. Similar to how there are communities built for young people on social media, there are also communities built for parents. By following Instagram or TikTok hashtags like #parenthood, #parenting tips, or #parentinggoals, you will gain access to a library of posts, images, and videos telling you what you supposedly need to know about raising your children.

A national poll published by the C.S. Mott Children's Hospital found that parents use social media for various reasons; a great majority of them enjoy discussing parenting topics, sharing their experiences, and looking for parenting advice (Clark & Woolford, 2023). The appeal of sourcing information from social media versus other outlets is that you get to hear different perspectives from professional doctors who have experience caring for mothers and children, as well as everyday mothers and fathers who have been in your situation.

Here's where things turn ugly: Chronic social media usage can cause you to value other people's opinions about parenting over trusting your gut instincts. Imagine hearing the message "If you're not homeschooling, you're not giving your child the best education" repeated 10 times a day by 10 different people. The first few days, you might scroll past it without thinking much about the message because it's not part of your value system. However, after weeks of being exposed to this message, you might feel intense pressure to rethink your decision to keep your children in traditional school. The message suggests that you might not be acting in the best interests of your children and that only homeschooling parents truly care about their children's future.

Besides overvaluing other people's opinions, chronic social media usage can also make you compare your parenting style with methods used by other parents. In the beginning, it could feel like admiration, and you might be inspired to adopt new strategies. For example, seeing a mother making bread, butter, and cakes in her kitchen might inspire you to improve your culinary skills so your family can enjoy fresh and healthy homemade meals. Over time, the admiration you felt at the beginning could turn into pressure to maintain a certain lifestyle. For example, instead of preparing homemade meals once in a while, you might expect yourself to do it every day because that's what the social media mother does.

The final stage is when the pressure morphs into self-doubt and resentment, usually when you struggle to handle the intense pressure. You might doubt that you have what it takes to nurture your children the *real* way (whatever that may be to you), and seeing other moms on social media achieving what you find difficult or demanding makes you feel inadequate in comparison. These comparisons can negatively impact your sense of self-worth, causing you to value yourself by what you can do for your family instead of the phenomenal parent and individual that you are.

What you learn after a while of being exposed to social media posts, images, and videos is that the content you see and engage with on social media platforms is either photoshopped or carefully curated to sell illusions of perfection. The perfection pressure cooker had already reached a boiling point before you got onto social media. All it took was repetitive exposure to the illusory content to brainwash you into believing that those standards were realistic and that you could achieve them. The good news is that breaking out of the illusion is possible by regulating your social media usage. Some of the boundaries you can work on include:

Create a Family Media Plan

A family media plan is a document that outlines rules around screen usage and limits at home. What's great about this is that the rules apply to all family members, from the oldest to the youngest, which fosters a sense of accountability. For example, if your children have screen curfews, then so do you. If phones aren't allowed to be used in certain areas of the house or during certain activities like mealtimes, you are expected to abide by those rules too. Creating a family media plan can help manage your social media usage, allowing you more time to be present with your family.

Lead by Example

Children are highly impressionable, especially when they are younger. They learn what acceptable and unacceptable behaviors look like by watching you closely. If you are chronically on social media, your children might be learning that it's okay to prioritize screen time over real interactions or to avoid meaningful communication and real-life responsibilities. Young girl children, in particular, might learn that it's okay to seek external validation and value themselves by how they appear to others. Take a moment to reflect on the positive beliefs and values you want to instill in your children and what behaviors might help you send those messages.

Engage in Offline Activities

Show your family that being immersed in the real world feels more fulfilling than being fixed on screens. Incorporate offline activities into your daily schedule that you can perform alone or with your loved ones. These activities can serve many purposes, such as helping you prioritize self-care, bond with your family, or improve your organizational skills and time management. Examples include gardening, cooking, reading, goal-setting, journaling, meditating, going to the gym, playing board games, and participating in creative hobbies.

Reassessing your relationship with social media allows you to regain control over your thoughts, emotions, and behaviors. Instead of making decisions based on the influence of other people, you can think deeply about what matters to you and what kind of environment you desire to create for your children. Being a mother or father means that you are an expert on parenting your children, regardless of whether you have a degree or not. Tuning out the noises from the public and tuning into your inner voice can help you become sensitive and even intuitive about your children's needs. Believe that you have the answers already inside you; you only need to pay attention and listen carefully for them.

Embracing Imperfection—Your Path to Freedom

If you ever find yourself trapped inside a "perfection pressure cooker," just know that there is a way out. You can intentionally challenge the social, cultural, and gender-based expectations that are imposed on you and decide on what you choose to believe and adopt in your household. What society won't tell you is that parenting is supposed to be messy because you are raising little humans who don't know how to think, feel, or behave unless they are taught through ongoing reinforcement.

On the other hand, you are still growing and learning about yourself as a parent and individual, and you won't always do things perfectly. Having grace for your children and yourself allows you to carve out your path to freedom that aligns with your family's needs and desired future. The following are sustainable strategies that can help you embrace your imperfections and feel greater confidence about your parenting duties:

Redefining "Good Parenting"

The saying that "it takes a village to raise a child" is true. The advice, guidance, and support you receive from your network can strengthen you during the valley moments of parenting. However, one specific piece of advice you cannot seek from others is how to be a good parent. Everyone has their own understanding of what good parenting entails, which is shaped by their past experiences and aspirations. What you might see as good parenting, someone else might criticize or suggest what they feel are better alternatives.

Added to this, the subject of "good" versus "bad" can create a moral dilemma. Here are questions to consider: if your parenting practices do not align with what society believes are good techniques, therefore making them "bad," does that mean you are a bad parent? Are you a bad parent for allowing your children to stay up past their bedtime on some days because other parents encourage bedtime schedules? Are you a bad parent for not worrying too much about your children's grades at school so long as they do their best and enjoy the process of learning?

There will be many instances on your parenting journey where the concept of "good parenting" seems ambiguous and downright inappropriate. It's up to you to either redefine what good parenting means in the context of your family or completely discard the concept. Whether you are labeled as a good parent or not doesn't change your status and the impact you have on your children's lives. Therefore, instead of focusing on being good, you can focus instead on having a positive influence on your children.

Learning From Mistakes

Parents are people who make mistakes just like anybody else. Some parents are overbearing, others fail to set boundaries, and a large number continue to allow their negative childhood experiences to affect how they relate to their children. But just because parents make mistakes doesn't mean they are not fit for the job. You can bounce back stronger from your mistakes if you choose to adjust your perspective about them. For instance, you can choose to view mistakes as detours rather than dead ends, which offers an opportunity to make different choices.

Learning from your mistakes begins by understanding what happened and what lessons you can take from the situation moving forward. Here are some questions you can reflect on after encountering various parenting challenges:

1. What did my child need from me at that moment?

2. Was I responding to my child's needs or reacting to my emotions?
3. Which of my own needs did I tune out at that moment?
4. How could I have expressed my needs better?
5. Have I set realistic expectations based on my child's age and abilities?
6. Are my expectations fair to me as a parent?
7. How can I manage my stress so it doesn't affect my parenting?
8. How can I model the behaviors I want to see in my child?

Finding Joy in the Journey

Mindfulness is an Eastern philosophy that has become popular in the West. It refers to the state of being present in the moment, completely focusing on what is happening here and now (Glembocki, 2023). Being mindful isn't something that occurs naturally, especially for parents with busy schedules. At any given moment, there could be hundreds of thoughts racing through your mind, preventing you from being anchored in the present moment.

Teaching yourself to be mindful allows you to embrace the highs and lows of parenting and accept your family situation for what it is rather than what you imagine it to be. Your life may not be perfect, but with greater acceptance of your circumstances, you can cultivate a genuine appreciation for what you have. There are a few ways that first-time parents can practice mindfulness, which could be:

- Fully engage with your child during everyday activities like feeding, bathing, talking, and playing. Make eye contact with them, use gentle touch to connect, and mimic their facial expressions.
- Listen to your child when they express their thoughts, even the long explanations that feel repetitive. Validate them by nodding your head, smiling, showing concern, or saying phrases like "I am listening" or "I understand what you mean."

- Stay calm during moments when your patience is tested. Practice self-soothing techniques like deep breathing exercises to reduce stress and manage your emotions.

There are also specific mindful strategies that apply to seasoned parents with more than one child, which include:

- Make a conscious effort to spend uninterrupted time with your children. Put your electronic devices away and engage in offline activities that encourage open communication and collaboration.

- Turn mundane daily tasks like driving your children to school or eating meals into mindful moments. Connect with your children by asking them open-ended questions, sharing stories, or simply enjoying the silence together.

- Practice self-compassion and model it in front of your children. This can teach them that it's okay to have bad days, make mistakes, or face obstacles in life. What matters aren't the challenges but your approach toward them. Practicing self-compassion allows you to adopt a positive attitude and parenting mindset.

Breaking free from the perfect parent trap requires awareness that you have slipped inside the metaphoric pressure cooker and have allowed the influence of the media, stereotypes, friends, and family to inform your role and responsibilities as a parent. You have a choice on whether to adhere to the expectations imposed by society or find your path to parenting freedom. Maintain your sovereignty by believing that you are the best person to raise your children because you brought them into this world. You have the answers to every parenting challenge inside of you—but you must drown out the noise from outside to hear them.

Chapter 2:

Unlocking the Mystery of Your Child's Behavior

There is usually an "inside" story to every "outside" behavior. Though we may not be able to know that "inside story," there's generally some inner reason for what children do. –Fred Rogers

Your Child Is Not Your Mirror

Watching your children grow can often feel like taking a walk down memory lane. With each milestone they reach, you are taken back to your childhood and reminisce about your "firsts," like your first birthday or the first sport you played. However, you are also reminded of the very different childhood you had and the painful experiences that you wouldn't want your children to live through.

It is normal to desire for your children to have a better upbringing than the one you had and to seize the opportunities presented to them. If you never got to play outside regularly, you might encourage your child to spend a lot of time playing outdoors. If you didn't perform well at school and therefore missed out on scholarships and other academic prizes, you might push your child to take their schooling seriously so they can achieve greater life outcomes than you did.

However, the trouble with this thinking is that it assumes your children are replicas of you, sharing the same thoughts, interests, needs, and aspirations as you. In reality, the only two things you share with your children are your genes and last name. Everything else about them is unique. Your children's uniqueness isn't noticeable in the early childhood years since they haven't reached the identity formation stage, which, according to Erik Erikson, happens between 12 and 18 years old (*Identity Development Theory*, 2022).

It also shouldn't surprise you when your older children start to explore their identities when they reach puberty and throughout their teenage years. During this phase of their lives, they may test boundaries, switch up their routines, experiment with fashion and beauty, and be drawn to different hobbies and peer groups. They could also "act out" and challenge your authority as a way to assert their values, beliefs, and independence.

None of the changes your children go through may reflect the type of adolescence and life you wanted for them. However, your children are not born to fulfill your childhood dreams or parenting vision. They were born to uncover their talents and gifts and leave their mark in this world. Whenever you project your fears, doubts, or regrets onto your children, they internalize those feelings and believe they aren't good enough to pursue their dreams. As a result, your children may settle for a "safe life" that pleases you as their parent but doesn't bring out the best version of who they are.

The Mini-Me Myth

The term "mini-me" comes from the movie, *Austin Powers*, where the antagonist, Dr. Evil, is followed around by his right-hand man named Mini-Me, who is the literal miniature version of him, down to his dress code and evil traits (Msingi Afrika Team, 2022). After the movie came out, it became a trend for some parents to call their children "mini-me" and dress up in the same outfits or rock the same hairstyles.

While this trend seems like harmless fun, there is an underlying tone of egotism that's associated with it. Unconsciously, parents who see their children as mini versions of themselves rob their little ones of expressing their own identities through their choice of clothing, interests, and hobbies. The children end up becoming caricatures of them and forgo discovering their distinct personalities, which creates confusion about their place in the world and who they are destined to be.

Parents who subscribe to the mini-me trend think of it as getting a second chance at being young again. Some might use this golden opportunity to relive or correct experiences from their past. For example, a mother who always dreamed of attending ballet lessons as a child but never got the chance to may ensure that her daughter attends lessons and becomes a ballerina, regardless of whether she enjoys ballet or not. Or a father who spent his childhood doing strenuous physical tasks against his will may be opposed to his son performing any kind of physical labor like house chores, even if his son expresses an interest in learning.

Understanding Individuality

Seeing your children as mini versions of you can restrict them from exploring the world on their own terms. You focus on protecting your children from your fears rather than teaching them how to navigate through life with courage and optimism. Additionally, the inability to see your children as separate individuals could create an unhealthy dynamic of enmeshment where you operate as one entity with one mind instead of separate entities with distinct minds.

Enmeshment refers to bonds between family members that lack boundaries and emotional independence (Porrey, 2023). There is no clear separation between the roles of parents and children, making it tough for children to recognize their individual needs and follow their own paths. In these families, parents may rely on their children for emotional support or groom their children into being excessively dependent on them. They may also treat their children as "friends" rather than children who need guidance and a good role model.

When they grow up, these children may experience various emotional issues that affect their sense of self and ability to forge healthy relationships with others. Some of the challenges they could face include:

- lack of self-trust and self-belief
- inability to carry out tasks independently
- unable to think for themselves
- rely on others for their emotional stability
- targeted by controlling or manipulative partners
- defining their self-worth by what others think of them
- people-pleasing tendencies to gain approval from others
- feeling guilty for pursuing goals that are unrelated to their family

If enmeshment is something that you are struggling with, you may have been raised in a family where the lines between parents and children were blurred. This is because enmeshment is a pattern of behavior that can be passed down from generation to generation.

For example, if your mother confided in you about her mature life dramas or romantic relationships—inappropriate information to share with a child—she may have blurred the boundaries of communication and normalized sharing deep and sensitive information with you. As a parent, you may find yourself doing the same with your children unconsciously, perpetuating the same pattern you learned as a child.

When you are enmeshed with your children, it can be difficult for you to watch them grow up and gain independence. Their ability to form a separate identity and express their individuality could feel threatening, as though they are abandoning you or being disloyal. However, this is not what is happening. Individuality means distinguishing yourself from others. It is a natural process that occurs from childhood to adulthood, during which your children announce to the world who they are.

Embracing individuality is a sign of high self-esteem and self-awareness. For your children to feel comfortable being distinct from others, they must have gained an understanding of their strengths, weaknesses, innate talents, and abilities. They accept who they are and don't allow what others think or feel to define them or influence their behaviors. In adulthood, they will learn to value their thoughts and opinions, solve problems creatively, and display resilience during setbacks.

By encouraging individuality from your children, you can significantly improve the quality of your relationships. Instead of being codependent on each other, you can become interdependent. In other words, your differences are no longer seen as a threat but opportunities to learn from each other and balance each other's strengths and weaknesses. Moreover, you play distinct roles as parent and child, which allows you to better serve one another's needs. Growth is also possible because neither of you gets in the way of the other's success; instead, each person leverages their talents and abilities to support the other.

Separating Identity From Behavior

Your children's individuality is something worthy of celebrating; however, that doesn't mean you will always be proud of their behaviors. Each child will have their own temperament, which refers to how they emotionally adapt to situations (American Academy of Pediatrics, 2024).

While temperaments can change with therapeutic interventions, they are mostly fixed ways that your children show up to the world. This is an important point to emphasize so that you don't stress yourself seeking to change who your children are. A better approach is to learn their temperaments and the factors influencing their temperaments, such as moods, intensity, attention span, stress tolerance, and sensory threshold.

For example, you might have an energetic child who needs frequent physical activity to feel balanced. Too little of this can make them feel restless and irritable, but too much can lead to overstimulation and impulsivity. You might have another child who has a low-stress tolerance and becomes easily upset with routine changes or when you use a harsh tone of voice to discipline them. They may also fear people and new situations that are unpredictable and can come across to others as withdrawn or anti-social.

In each of the scenarios above, the children's temperaments determine how they approach different situations. Sometimes, they may respond well, and other times, they may have a hard time processing what's happening. Making quick judgments of your children's temperaments, especially when they are going through a difficult time can make you mistakenly confuse their behaviors for their identity. For example, when your hyperactive child throws objects because they're overstimulated, you might see their actions as stubbornness or rebelliousness.

Teachers at school infamously make this mistake. They often make snap judgments about students' characters based on their academic performance or classroom temperament. Students who follow instructions and remain focused in the classroom are seen as intelligent and motivated learners. However, those with a short attention span and poor self-regulation skills could be unfairly perceived as unintelligent and unmotivated.

It takes mindful awareness to separate your child from their behaviors. At times, you may need to take 30 minutes to process your emotions and objectively assess the situation so you can see the distinction. Your children's temperaments won't always be appropriate, but that doesn't make them bad children.

Communicating this message to them is essential too. Whenever one of your children misbehaves, let them know that you are not happy with their behavior, but you believe they can make better choices next time because they are smart and know better. These words allow them to see that while their behavior has gotten them in trouble, their behavior does not limit them, and they can rise above it.

Managing Expectations Through Objective Parenting

In the long term, you may need to work on managing your expectations of your children to ensure that their behaviors and temperaments don't get in the way of building strong and positive relationships. One of the ways to do this is through adopting an objective parenting style.

In her book titled *The Baby Whisperer Solves All Your Problems*, British nurse and author Tracy Hogg describes how subjective and objective parenting impacts parents' approach to children's behaviors (Hogg & Blau, 2006). Subjective parents react based on their emotions; and how they feel about what happened. In contrast, objective parents react based on the situation at hand; and what their children may be signaling or need from them.

To illustrate these parenting styles, consider a situation where a five-year-old throws a tantrum while shopping with their parent at a grocery store. The subjective parent feels embarrassed about their child's behavior and threatens to leave without paying for their candy if they don't calm down. They are more concerned about how their child's behavior impacts them than what the behavior might signal about their child's needs.

The objective parent, on the other hand, sees the tantrum and thinks about what triggers their child may have been exposed to. Their focus is on understanding what caused the behavior to take place and how they can soothe their upset child. The tantrum is seen as a sign of distress rather than attention-seeking behavior, and therefore the root cause must be found and addressed.

When your children's temperaments become challenging, remind yourself to be objective when assessing the situation. Understandably, you are human, and putting your emotions aside won't always be easy. But if possible, delay making any decisions or communicating with them until you have your emotions under control. Remind yourself that your children's behaviors are not personal, but instead indications of how they are feeling. If your child gives you the silent treatment, for example, they are reacting from a place of hurt inside of them.

Being curious about what might have hurt them can help you uncover the needs behind their silent treatment. Perhaps they don't feel heard, and giving the silent treatment is a form of protest to get you to listen. When the answers are not obvious, ask questions or observe their body language to understand what they might be thinking or feeling. For example, younger children will use nagging to seek your attention while older children use isolation to express their disapproval. Start documenting your children's non-verbal behaviors and what they mean so that you can gain insight into their troubling behaviors.

What's *REALLY* Going On? Decoding Their Behavior

Ten-year-old Max had been acting out for weeks—arguing with his siblings, slamming doors, and refusing to do his homework. His parents thought that he was just being difficult, but one evening, after an emotional outburst, he broke down and admitted he was being bullied at school. Every day, classmates would tease him about his appearance, leaving him feeling alone and insecure. His acting out was due to built-up frustration that he didn't know how to release appropriately. Once his parents understood what was happening, they were able to intervene and support him.

Children do not have the same cognitive and emotional skills as grown adults because their mental processing isn't as developed. Therefore, how they solve social and emotional problems won't always make sense to you as an adult. For instance, little Max could have called his parents or teachers aside to address the bullying. That would've been the logical thing to do. However, expecting that level of maturity and level-headedness from a 10-year-old isn't realistic.

There is more to your children's behaviors than what meets the eye, so try not to take their actions personally. What comes across as disrespect could be hiding the need for validation, or what seems like laziness could really be fear of change or difficulty managing transitions. You owe it to your children to be more responsive and less reactive when decoding their behaviors. Since they don't have the words to eloquently express their feelings, you'll need to do the detective work and get to the bottom of the issue.

The Basics of Child Development

Were you aware that acting out is a natural part of a child's development? Doctors don't call them the "Terrible Twos" or "Threenagers" for nothing. Particularly during the early years, children have no sense of right and wrong, and even when they are somewhat aware of what's expected of them, they can test the boundaries out of curiosity to see what might happen.

Small children are also egotistical, although this is an essential survival mechanism for them. Without strong cognitive, emotional, and social skills, they rely on how they feel to determine their security. Slight discomfort like a soiled diaper or not getting things done their way can trigger extreme reactions like crying, screaming, or hitting. Essentially, they are looking out for their needs and making sure Mom or Dad doesn't forget about them.

Acting out is normal during adolescence too. The combination of hormone imbalances, identity exploration, and managing peer relationships can cause significant stress and anxiety for teenagers, especially when they haven't learned healthy coping strategies. Instead of identifying, accepting, and communicating their thoughts and emotions, they might argue with family members, violate rules, and engage in risk-taking behaviors.

Research shows that offensive teen behaviors peak during mid-to-late adolescence and steadily decline in the twenties (Jafarian & Ananthakrishnan, n.d.). No serious intervention like counseling is needed unless the behavior is concerning for the following reasons:

- **The behavior is out of character for your child.** Every child has parameters regarding how far they will go to express their disapproval. When your child does something that isn't typical of them, it can be helpful to seek advice from a professional to figure out why they are behaving that way.

- **The behavior is happening more frequently.** Breaking the rules every now and then isn't worrisome, but when it happens regularly, or after specific situations, there could be more behind those actions. If your child is not comfortable opening up to you about their motivations, they can speak to a family member they trust or a school counselor.

- **The behavior is interfering with your child's everyday life.** Troublesome behaviors that are uncontrollable, intense, disruptive, or take time to subside can start to interfere with your child's focus, moods, productivity, and cooperativeness. Eventually, they may experience challenges at school, at home, or when making friends. Seeking expert support can offer your child the relief they deserve.

Emotional Triggers

Emotional triggers are internal and external cues that evoke strong feelings in your child (Darcy, 2022). Internal cues could be things like intrusive thoughts, memories, or negative self-talk. External cues could be unexpected transitions, rejection, failure, or being exposed to certain sounds, lights, smells, or expressions. When these triggers occur, they activate your child's stress response, putting them into a state of fight-flight-freeze. During this state, they tend to lose their ability to think rationally about how to navigate the situation. Instead, they may follow their urges and impulses.

One key characteristic of emotional triggers is that the reaction doesn't match the situation. Almost always, the decisions or behaviors carried out after the trigger is set off are exaggerated or don't make sense for the situation. Thus, it can be beneficial to identify your children's triggers—and help them identify them too—so they have a few seconds to pause, recognize they are triggered, and take a different course of action. Below are common emotional triggers your children may experience:

- **Feeling ignored or unheard:** Nobody wants to feel like what they have to say or think doesn't matter. When your child isn't getting the attention they desire from you, they may become angry.

- **Going through change and transitions:** Children, particularly those who have anxiety or are on the autistic spectrum, could feel caught off guard and frustrated whenever they have to move from one task to another or experience unexpected changes to their routine.

- **Difficulty completing tasks:** Some children have a hard time accepting when they can't complete a task, like tying their shoelaces or figuring out a math problem. They become angry with themselves and may have an outburst.

- **Separation from parents:** Separation anxiety is a real experience that can trigger some children to feel sad and abandoned. This normally happens with younger children; however, it can affect older children too.

- **Overstimulation:** Sensory overloads like being exposed to bright lights, loud noises, overcrowded places, pungent smells, or prickly fabrics can trigger children to have meltdowns. Older children can also be overstimulated when they don't have proper time management skills or when they have too many tasks to complete within a short period.

At times, you'll be lucky to see triggers coming to help your children manage their stress and calm down. Other times, you might catch the triggers when it's too late, and your children have begun emotionally unraveling. What you can do to train yourself to recognize your children's triggers is to write down the details of how previous triggers unfolded. Over time, these details will reveal patterns of how your children respond in certain situations. Here are the important things to note:

- What happened?
- What happened immediately before and after?
- What time of day did it happen?
- Who was there when it happened?
- Were there unmet biological needs (e.g., tiredness, hunger)?
- Were there unmet emotional needs (e.g., attention, affection)?

Communication Beyond Words

Our children communicate through verbal and non-verbal language. As parents, we need to teach ourselves how to "read between the lines" and decode the messages our kids are sending to us with their facial expressions, gestures, tone of voice, or body language. It's important to note that each child will have their way of communicating with you non-verbally, and their signals may not look the same as the signals given by other children.

For example, one of your children might avoid eye contact when they are guilty of doing something wrong. Another child might avoid eye contact when they are feeling vulnerable. You may also have a child who expresses anger by raising their voice and another child who expresses anger by keeping silent. You need to study each child and learn the ways that they use non-verbal communication to express themselves. Think of this as a fun challenge of getting to know your children better. Every time you guess the intention behind their non-verbal cues correctly, reward yourself. When you guess wrong, be more attentive the next time it happens.

Don't be shy to ask your children questions to gain more clarity about what they are attempting to communicate with you through their non-verbal language. For example, you might say "Hey buddy, I noticed you didn't greet me when you came downstairs this morning. Is everything okay?" or "You haven't talked much the whole day. Is there something on your mind?"

To maintain transparency and model effective communication, be willing to express the needs behind your non-verbal cues. For example, you might tell your children, "I'm sitting quietly right now because I'm feeling overwhelmed and need a little space to think. Once I feel better, we can talk about what's going on." This not only explains your non-verbal behavior but also shows your children how to manage their emotions by taking a pause when needed.

Empathy in Action

When your children have a fight-or-flight approach to solving problems, responding to them with the same approach will only escalate the issue. When they are emotional and impulsive, they need your loving and nurturing presence to ground them. Empathy refers to imagining trading places with someone else and experiencing their reality. Doing this enables you to understand the big "why" behind their behaviors.

Difficult children need empathy just as much as easy children do. Their temperament and expressions may not be socially acceptable, but that doesn't mean they don't deserve consideration and compassion. To show empathy to your children, you must have an awareness that they are separate individuals who see the world differently from you. Be open and curious about learning from your children's outlook and experiences so that you can understand the incredible beings they are.

Parenting with empathy can look like:

- **Actively listening to your child when they speak.** Put away your cell phone or reading book and look your child in the eyes. Connect with the words coming out of their mouths and the subtle expressions shown on their face and body. Listen without interrupting them, then paraphrase what you heard at the end. For instance, you might say, "It sounds like that English paper went well. I'm happy to hear that!"

- **Acknowledge and name your child's emotions.** Help your child identify their emotions and work through them. Many times, children are aware they are in a bad mood but could be confused as to why. You might say, "It seems like you're disappointed that your friend canceled the play date. That must feel annoying." Not only are you teaching your child emotion vocabulary, but you are also showing them that it's okay to embrace strong emotions.

- **Offer reassurance and support.** When your child is going through a difficult time, remind them they are not alone. Whether they are ready to speak to you about their challenges or not, you will always be there to hear them out and offer encouraging words. You can reassure them by saying, "No matter what problems you face, I'll always be here to listen and offer a hug. We'll get through this together."

Empathy is a way to strengthen your relationships with your children and connect on a heart level. It also allows you to open up about your feelings and let your children see that you can relate to the experiences they go through. Some of the most meaningful conversations you will have with your children start with approaching them with empathy. Even if you disapprove of their behaviors, your empathy makes them feel seen and valued.

Recognizing that you have a different outlook on life than your children helps you separate your needs from theirs and understand where they are coming from. How your children behave has everything to do with them and very little to do with you. Lean in and show curiosity about decoding their behaviors and the intent behind them. Be mindful of factors like their developmental stage or emotional triggers, which could influence their behaviors. Most importantly, work on managing your expectations and leading with empathy so you can accept your children for the unique individuals they are, not who you desire them to be.

Chapter 3:

You and Your Emotions Matter Too

If we don't shape our kids, they will be shaped by outside forces that don't care what shape our kids are in. –Dr. Louise Hart

Permission to Feel: Why Your Emotions Are Valid

The journey of parenting follows the same patterns as the weather outside. There are days when the dark clouds of worrying thoughts or frustrations come over us, and we don't feel like getting out of bed or fit to carry on. Eventually, those clouds pass, and the warmth of our radiant attitudes, hopes, and milestones comfort us, giving us the inner strength to keep going.

Intense emotions of anger, sadness, betrayal, or disappointment are natural to experience as a parent. These feelings may not be directed at your child or children but at the circumstances that impact your parenting, such as work troubles, relationship stress, health issues, financial insecurity, and so on.

Even though society expects you to be strong 24/7, the reality is that you have a stress and pain threshold, like anybody else, and after some time, the increasing pressures you face can cause emotional distress. It's important to give yourself permission to explore your emotional life beyond the pleasant feelings of happiness and gratitude. Allow yourself to embrace your fears, guilt, shame, and resentment.

Something remarkable happens when you allow yourself to feel: You develop emotional resilience that helps you navigate through parenting hardships without collapsing under pressure. Your emotions are only overpowering when you refuse to confront them because they seem bigger and scarier than they actually are. Shifting your awareness to your emotions enables you to put them in perspective, challenge your emotions-based assumptions, and regain control of your life's narrative.

The Myth of the Selfless Parent

A few years ago, a friend of mine told me about a story when her husband was preparing her morning coffee, and their daughter remarked, "No, Dad, don't make it too hot. Mom likes her coffee cold." She found this funny because her daughter had been observing her habit of drinking cold coffee due to her attending to everyone's needs before taking a seat at the table and enjoying her beverage.

Our parental altruism is what makes our duties as parents one-of-a-kind. No other role operates on endless service without seeking recognition or compensation. Selflessness is about being concerned with the needs of others more than your own. Some of us perform selfless parenting so well that our children and spouses start to think that's part of our personalities and preferences.

The truth, however, is that selflessness without boundaries leads to exploitation. Your loved ones become accustomed to withdrawing love, support, service, and caregiving until they feel satisfied. Think of a young kid going to a candy store and being told they can take as much candy as they desire. Will they stop once their hands are full? Absolutely not. They will find ways of stashing candy in their pockets, jackets, and under their belts.

Giving your children unlimited access to your time, energy, money, and labor (both emotional and physical) creates a sense of entitlement around your precious resources. Indeed, you want to support your children in every way you can, but it's also wise to be honest about what you can and cannot do. Giving your children the impression that nothing is impossible or too much for you will only raise their expectations and demands. More importantly, it gives them a false idea of what healthy relationships built on reciprocity and consideration look like.

Alternative Parenting Approaches

Selfless parents adopt what's known as permissive parenting. This parenting style discourages enforcing rules or structures that might limit children in any way. They can think, feel, and act how they choose without experiencing the consequences. Selfless parents end up taking on responsibilities that their children are supposed to handle, such as feeding or bathing themselves or completing their homework. They also solve problems for their children and give in to their requests to avoid negative emotions (Nelson, 2023).

The long-term impact of permissive parenting is raising children who display poor self-regulation and decision-making abilities. Due to the lack of a predictable structure at home and reassuring goals to strive for, they may be prone to self-esteem and delinquency issues. Selfless parents who desire to prepare their children to succeed in life must give them more sense of stability and security, which comes in the form of rules and standards.

Authoritative and positive parenting are two alternative parenting styles that provide warmth and nurturing while enforcing structure. Authoritative parenting seeks to bring out the best in children by giving them clear parameters to function (Nelson, 2023). They are taught the difference between acceptable and unacceptable behavior and given explanations regarding why one is more desirable than the other. Consequences for bad behaviors are also discussed and enforced with appropriate measures. Authoritative parents see their children as collaborators rather than rulers of the home or subordinates. They talk to them with respect, encourage negotiation, and value their opinions.

Positive parenting uses positive reinforcement, such as praise and recognition to teach children desirable attitudes, beliefs, and behaviors (Harvey, 2015). The focus is on highlighting the good instead of emphasizing the bad to raise children's confidence. When children believe they can improve their behaviors, they are more willing to try. Similar to authoritative parenting, rules and consequences are discussed in a low-stress environment and children are aware of what's expected of them. Open communication and empathy are encouraged to better understand the intentions and needs behind children's behaviors.

By adopting either authoritative or positive parenting, selfless parents can protect themselves from over-giving to their own detriment. They can teach their children to take ownership of their behaviors, play their unique role in the family, and become sensitive to the needs of other family members, making sure everyone feels valued and supported.

The Power of Acknowledgement

Parents often put up a tough exterior to others and suppress their emotions. Even behind closed doors, some may struggle to let their emotions come to the surface. There are reasons to explain this, such as growing up in a family that didn't support emotional expression or being trapped in the pressure cooker of societal expectations. In the long run, the inability to acknowledge and accept emotions can lead to burnout, resentment, negative self-talk, or internalized shame.

It's good emotional hygiene to find healthy outlets for releasing intense emotions. A healthy outlet could be someone you trust, like your spouse or best friend, or your favorite creative hobby that helps you offload stress. Please note that your children are not outlets for venting your frustrations. Regardless of how old they might be, their job is not to counsel you about the various problems you are dealing with.

Emotionally depending on your children is a form of role reversal where they take on parenting duties and guide you as though you were their child. This creates an unhealthy dynamic in your parent-child relationships and unfairly causes your children to mature too quickly and feel responsible for taking care of you.

Beyond finding healthy outlets, you can acknowledge your emotions by taking ownership of them. Using a simple phrase like "I feel therefore I need" allows you to take what seems like a big and uncontrollable emotion and manage it. There is also something liberating about naming whatever you are feeling; you realize that you are separate from your emotions and don't need to be held down by them.

Here are some phrases that you can practice saying to acknowledge your emotions:

- "I feel frustrated when the kitchen is a mess; therefore, I need everyone to clean up after themselves."
- "I feel anxious about the upcoming doctor's visit; therefore, I need us to sit down and plan together."
- "I feel taken for granted when I'm always the one planning family activities; therefore, I need to see mutual effort and cooperation."
- "I feel tired when I get back home from work; therefore, I need at least 20 minutes alone before I start preparing dinner."
- "I feel disappointed when you do something I asked you not to do; therefore, I need us to rehash boundaries."

Emotional Intelligence for Parents

Emotional intelligence can be defined as the awareness of your emotions and the emotions of others (Travers, 2024). Some skills that build emotional intelligence include self-awareness, self-regulation, empathy, social awareness, and relationship management. By understanding your thoughts and emotions, you can better control them and be sensitive to how they impact those around you, particularly your partner and children.

First-time parents and seasoned parents go through emotional turbulences as part of their normal parenting experiences. One example of an emotional time is after childbirth when both mothers and fathers go through "baby blues." Due to the rush of hormones, sleep deprivation, adjusting to their new identities, or adapting to environmental changes, both parents can feel symptoms of anxiety, sadness, and depression. When these symptoms continue for weeks, they can lead to postpartum depression (Chisholm, 2017).

Other examples of times when you might experience emotional instability are during major life transitions and changes, such as starting a new job or changing careers, losing a parent, going through a divorce, having small children starting school, facing health scares and issues, experiencing financial problems, or adding a new child to your family. Displaying emotional intelligence isn't a cure for your stress, anxiety, or depression, and it certainly won't solve every problem. However, making this mindset shift can improve how you cope with challenges and approach parenting.

You may be wondering what emotionally intelligent parenting looks like. Two characteristics of emotionally intelligent parents make them handle stressful situations differently. The first is that they are conscientious, meaning they are intentional about doing things well (Travers, 2024). Whether they are preparing breakfast or driving their children to school, they feel responsible for doing what's right, regardless of their moods. Being conscientious allows emotionally intelligent parents to commit to their goals and routines and maintain a standard for how they interact with their kids. Of course, they may still have bad days, but the ups and downs of their emotions don't compromise the order and structure they have built.

To become more conscientious, you can practice the following habits:
- Set personal standards for yourself as a parent that are both fair and reasonable, then hold yourself accountable to them.
- Follow through on what you have said you will do, even if it means having a slow start. Avoid making promises to your children that you can't keep.

- Be intentional about spending time with your children. Schedule family activities once a day or a few times a week and ensure that you are bonding.
- Be consistent with enforcing rules and consequences; how you discipline your children today should be the same tomorrow. Post the rules around the house for greater transparency.

The second characteristic is agreeableness, which is the quality of cooperating with others. Agreeable parents are open-minded, flexible, compassionate, and willing to compromise (Travers, 2024). For instance, when they are presented with new information, they can change their minds and take a different approach. In contrast, parents who are disagreeable would hold firmly to their convictions even after they have been proven wrong. During conflicts, agreeable parents seek to understand their children's perspectives without judgment, which in turn makes their children feel comfortable opening up and expressing themselves. They are also willing to find a middle ground so that everyone can walk away feeling satisfied with the outcomes of the discussion.

Here are some parenting practices that can help you enhance agreeableness:

- Practice listening to your children attentively to understand the messages they are conveying through verbal and non-verbal language.
- Delay your reactions purposefully so that you can acknowledge and validate your children's experiences.
- Focus on solutions rather than emphasizing mistakes. Work together with your children to brainstorm creative ideas to address recurring problems.
- Use positive reinforcement like praise and affirmations to show appreciation for your children and encourage desirable behaviors.

Communicating Needs Within the Family

Having needs and being needy are two separate things. Most parents think they are being needy when they express to their children that they need help with house chores or ask their extended relatives for support in taking care of their children. In reality, they are simply leaning on their support system. Relationships are supposed to be based on reciprocity, the balance of giving and taking. When they become one-sided, one person ends up doing most of the giving, and the other does most of the taking, creating an unhealthy dynamic.

The next time you hold back from communicating your needs with your family, remind yourself that givers deserve to take some time. You aren't asking for too much when you make requests from your loved ones. The consequence of not speaking up and voicing your needs is that you create an inconvenience for yourself when help is available. It's like choosing to walk to the shops in the rain when you have a car parked outside. Moreover, you could hold silent grudges with loved ones who aren't aware of your unspoken needs. In the long term, this passive-aggressive approach can put a strain on your relationships and isolate you.

The Art of Constructive Expression

Communicating your needs can be tough because it requires a great deal of vulnerability. The possibility of being rejected or dismissed exists, regardless of how well you articulate your needs. At the end of the day, you cannot control how someone else responds to your needs, but you can control how effectively you communicate them. Instead of focusing on what they might think or feel about what you have to say, work on improving your delivery.

Below is a table showing the difference between positive and negative self-expression. Go through each example and notice how one response is constructive while the other is destructive. You can also read the expressions aloud to notice how differently they make you feel.

Situation	Positive self-expression (constructive)	Negative self-expression (destructive)
Feeling overwhelmed with responsibilities	"I feel overwhelmed with everything going on; therefore, I need some help with chores so we can work together."	"I can't handle everything on my own. No one ever helps me!"
Needing personal time	"I feel exhausted right now; therefore, I need a few minutes to myself to recharge, and then we can talk."	"I'm too tired to deal with you right now. Just leave me alone!"
Child arguing over rules	"I feel stressed when we argue about the rules, so I need us to sit down and calmly discuss them together."	"You always fight me on everything! Why can't you just listen?"
Handling a child's tantrum	"I feel stressed when you scream; therefore, I need you to use your words to tell me what's wrong."	"Stop screaming right now! I can't take it anymore!"
Wanting to spend quality time with loved ones	"I feel disconnected lately, so I need us to spend some time together as a family this weekend."	"We never spend time together anymore. No one cares about family time."

From the table above, you will notice that constructive self-expression involves taking ownership of your feelings and allowing your family members inside your inner world. You take the time to explain what you are going through and the impact of your situation so that they can see where you're coming from. Destructive self-expression shifts blame onto others, making them responsible for your feelings. It also uses exaggerations like "never" or "always," which magnify the problem and trigger the listener to get into a defensive position.

Emotional Honesty With Children

Constructive expression aims to model emotional honesty in front of your family. Emotional honesty is the ability to express your emotions without fear of judgment or criticism. It helps you feel at ease having difficult conversations where disagreements may occur. It's often thought that children are terrified of opening up to their parents, but parents are equally terrified of being vulnerable with their children. We are taking an emotional risk when we bear our souls and allow others into our inner world. All we want is for them to validate our experiences and make us feel heard and seen.

Cultivating emotional honesty starts with creating an emotionally safe home environment. Introduce values like tolerance of differences and compassion to teach your children how to accept thoughts and feelings that are different from theirs. For example, an older child could be taught to be tolerant of their younger sibling's nagging and understand that they may need extra attention from their family members. Tolerance and compassion around different temperaments are also key. Instead of thinking someone is "strange" for handling stress a different way or displaying different behaviors socially, you can teach your family to see those differences as normal and acceptable.

Emotional honesty can entail having heart-to-heart conversations with your children. These conversations need to be age-appropriate to ensure that mature or sensitive information isn't disclosed. It's never too early to start these conversations since young children from the age they start talking may have questions about hard topics like your family dynamic, the death of a loved one, or expectations about the future. To help you provide age-appropriate explanations, you can read children's books with life lessons or use toys and props to make illustrations.

When you don't know much about a specific topic that has been brought up by your child (e.g., LGBTQIA+ rights, alternatives to college, paranormal activities), you can go on a fact-finding mission together, watch a video, ask another family member, or speak to an expert.

Conflict Resolution and Emotional Repair

Relationships without conflict don't exist. Every now and then, your children might act out, or your partner might not be as supportive as you would like them to be. However, even during those tense moments, open communication is essential. Don't fall into the trap of going silent or pretending to be okay, as this invalidates your experience and makes it difficult to repair the affected relationships.

Below is a conflict resolution technique called DESO that you can learn and teach to your family (*Assertive Communication: The DESO Framework*, 2020). Whenever conflict ensues and hard conversations need to be had, use the DESO technique to structure your messages constructively and respectfully.

D—Describe

Start by describing the situation objectively. Focus on the events that took place which made you feel offended. For example, "Yesterday, you slammed the door in my face while I was trying to resolve an issue with you."

E—Express

Once you have described the situation, explain how it made you feel. Here, taking ownership of your emotions is necessary so the other person doesn't feel responsible for them. For example, "I felt hurt because I didn't deserve to be treated that way."

S—Specify

Specify what you want to see happen to repair the relationship emotionally. When making your request, be mindful of who you are asking and what you are asking for. It should be a request within the person's capacity to fulfill. For example, "Next time, please let me know when you are feeling emotionally overwhelmed so we can go our separate ways and take a break to calm down."

O—Outcome

Explain the benefits of honoring your request. In other words, what's in it for both of you? When the benefits outweigh the consequences, there is a greater motivation to adopt the new behavior. For example, "By doing this, we can end the conversation on good terms and feel positive about picking it up again later."

Besides resolving conflict, the DESO technique can be used to set boundaries with your family members. Nothing changes, except for the situation (boundary violation) that is described at the beginning. Practice the DESO technique with your children using relatable examples like not following the house rules or fighting with their siblings, so they feel prepared about what to do when they encounter those situations.

Parents are human too. They go through life's ups and downs just like their children. However, many parents struggle to accept their emotions and communicate their needs. By cultivating emotional intelligence and embracing vulnerability, they can open themselves up and allow their children inside their inner world. This act of courage could potentially inspire their children to feel comfortable exploring their emotions and expressing themselves without fear of judgment.

Chapter 4:

Living Your Dream While Raising a Family

Time is really the only capital that any human has and the only thing he can't afford to lose. –Thomas A. Edison

Keeping Your Fire Alive

Having children changes your approach to life, such as the things you value and the goals you want to pursue. The fact of the matter is that you are responsible for other human beings, so providing a comfortable life for them becomes your top priority. Your identity, beliefs, and lifestyle choices before being a parent fall by the wayside to make room for this new important role you will play.

It can be difficult to convince first-time parents to hold onto the interests and passions they enjoyed before becoming parents. They may take it as being neglectful of their parenting duties or failing to grow up and embrace their current life stage. However, that couldn't be further from the truth. Ask any seasoned parent whether interests and passions get in the way of parenting, and they'll tell you they don't. Parenting is a 24-hour, 7-days-a-week job, whereas hobbies occur for an hour or so a few times a month.

They'll also tell you that the idea of "growing up" is a myth we are fed by society. Inside every parent lives an inner child that represents their creative, imaginative, and youthful energy. The inner child is excitable, adventurous, playful, and curious. They love to explore the world, develop skills, and work toward materializing their dreams.

Every parent's inner child comes out to play when engaging in tasks and activities that awaken the fire inside them. Think of a mother who just discovered sewing and now watches sewing tutorials on YouTube religiously, feeling more accomplished as she learns advanced techniques. Or a father who has been obsessed with cars since he was a little boy and now gets a thrill whenever he visits car dealerships or attends car shows and racing events.

You tend to encourage your children to play, but when will you make time for play? You may never get started if your parenting duties are your excuse for not finding meaningful pursuits or chasing your dreams. Parenting is a full-time job with no rest days; there will never be a "perfect time" to prioritize leisure because the demands of being a parent don't stop. So, what will you do? Wait until your children leave for college? Perhaps by then, there will be other roles you have taken on that fill up your schedule.

Awakening your inner fire through venturing into the unknown and exploring your interests allows you to reconnect with parts of yourself that you have abandoned since becoming a parent. You deserve to have fun, be creative, learn new skills, and set personal goals for yourself.

Doing these things won't conflict with your parenting duties—if anything, they will help you manage stress, build relationships, and increase personal fulfillment.

Identifying Your Passions

You might be ready and willing to find a passion outside of parenting but don't know what you're passionate about. This is a common experience that parents go through and nothing to be embarrassed about. We often imagine passions as extraordinary projects that either make us a lot of money or consume all of our time. Truthfully, they don't have to be any of those things.

A passion can be whatever your mind gravitates in the stillness of the day or at night when you are struggling to fall asleep. It's that goal that you spontaneously think about every few months and tell yourself, "One day..." or that task that everyone keeps complimenting you about that you perform effortlessly. A passion could also be that one subject that you could host a TED Talk on because of how much you love it. Some passions can be monetized, but that's not why you get into it. What motivates you to find and nurture your passions is the sense of freedom, contentment, and purpose it brings.

What's Your Passion Quiz

Finding your passions requires paying attention to your thoughts, emotions, behaviors, and physical sensations. Notice what tasks and activities you think about often, feel attracted to, or energize you. Passion carries the same energy as love, so examine what you love to do, talk to others about, or fantasize about.

The following quiz is a fun and interactive way of helping you reflect on your daily life so you can identify where your passions lie. Go through the multiple choice questions and answer them truthfully, then total your scores and analyze your results.

1. What activities make you lose track of time?

    A) Reading or writing

B) Working on hands-on projects

   C) Engaging in physical activities

   D) Helping others or giving advice

2. When you were younger, what did you dream of becoming?

   A) An author or artist

   B) An inventor or engineer

   C) An athlete or performer

   D) A teacher or counselor

3. What type of challenges do you enjoy solving?

   A) Creative or artistic challenges

   B) Technical or mechanical problems

   C) Physical or endurance challenges

   D) Emotional or relational issues

4. Which of these brings you the most satisfaction?

   A) Creating something new

   B) Fixing or improving something

   C) Achieving a physical goal

   D) Making a positive impact on someone's life

5. If you could dedicate your life to one thing without worrying about money, what would it be?

   A) Writing a novel or painting

   B) Building innovative products

   C) Training for a sport or adventure

   D) Volunteering or mentoring

Analyze your results:

- **Mostly A's:** Your passion likely lies in creative pursuits. Explore careers or hobbies in writing, art, music, or design.

- **Mostly B's:** You're drawn to innovation and problem-solving. Consider fields like engineering, technology, or hands-on projects.
- **Mostly C's:** You thrive in physical activities. Look into careers in sports, fitness, or any physically demanding field.
- **Mostly D's:** You find fulfillment in helping others. Consider roles in education, counseling, or community service.

After completing the quiz, spend another 20-30 minutes researching hobbies related to your results. For example, if you scored mostly C's, you can research active hobbies suitable for your lifestyle. Get some leads and make phone calls to studios, instructors, or fitness clubs. Find out what you'll need to get started and when you can join a class.

The intention is to ride on this momentum created by the quiz and take the first step. You might change your mind about the hobby after the first session, which is okay. Time to move on and try another one until you eventually find something that awakens that fire!

Balancing Dreams and Duties

Something I have heard repeated by moms is "How do I juggle raising kids and pursuing my career?" Ironically, not many fathers have this thought because traditionally caregiving is seen as the mother's responsibility. The phenomenon of "mom guilt" is a real thing. It describes the constant feeling of not doing enough to care for your children (Rooney, 2023).

Women feel the pressure to achieve a balance between work and home. However, it doesn't stop there. They feel the need to be the best at each role they play—the best wife, mother, cook, friend, daughter, employee, and so on. Once again, we find ourselves submerged in this pressure cooker of expectations that aren't fair or realistic. Think about it: with only 24 hours in a day (5-7 of those spent sleeping), how possible is it to "have it all?"

Subscribing to the 50/50 work-life balance concept harms your mental and emotional well-being and gives you a false sense of how much time you have in a day. Most days, the more realistic ratio would be 30/70, 80/20, or 10/90. Depending on your needs and priorities (which are ever-changing) and the amount of support you have at home and at work, you may lean toward focusing on personal tasks or workplace tasks.

For parents who work and have side hustles or passions, the ratio looks different. Instead of splitting your focus into two major areas of your life, you would split it into three, such as 30/30/50 or 40/40/20. The point is that there won't be a time when you feel like you are doing enough in each area of your life; however, by setting goals and giving yourself a reasonable timeframe to work with, you will see progress in all areas of your life.

Time Management Basics for Busy Parents

Effective time management helps you merge different aspects of your life without focusing solely on one. For instance, you could start your morning by setting intentions, taking your children to school, stopping by the local gym for a class, and then heading home to do some cleaning, meal prepping, and marketing tasks for your online business—all of this is achieved within the first half of your day.

Being busy shouldn't get in the way of your productivity. But understandably, there are only so many tasks you can schedule in 24 hours. Instead of thinking about what to add to your day, think instead about what might slow you down or cause distractions that you can cancel out. Removing items on your to-do list gives you more time to distribute to the things that matter to you. The aim is to focus on quality not quantity.

Here are some examples of things that waste precious time in your day that need to be removed to improve your time management:

- **Excessive social media scrolling:** An hour on social media feels like a few minutes. Mindlessly browsing through social media preoccupied your mind with news and trends that don't add value to your day. Yes, it's enjoyable, but only for a few hours at a time, preferably after you have gotten the productive tasks out of the way.

- **Perfectionism in household chores:** Cleaning your home is a productive and therapeutic task, but up to a certain point. When you tend to complete every chore perfectly, you can spend hours completing a task only meant to take you several minutes. Focus on "good enough" when it comes to cleaning and delegate some chores to your family members.

- **Overscheduling your children's activities:** As a parent, you are also the chauffeur and chaperone of your children to their various extracurricular activities. Set boundaries around how many activities each child can take on and how many times a week they can play. Copy their schedules onto a family calendar so that you can address overlaps and organize your day accordingly. If you have a partner, share the responsibility to transport your children to and from their activities so that you can have days of rest.

- **Unnecessary errands:** You don't have to leave the house for every errand. Some tasks can be done on apps, such as stocking up on groceries and getting them delivered to your door. If you need to leave the house, pick a day when you can complete your weeks' worth of errands.

- **Overthinking minor decisions:** A silent time waster is overthinking. You go around in circles in your head, contemplating whether or not to carry out a decision. In the end, you get trapped in the analysis stage and never get around to taking action. Tell yourself this: If it's not an immediate "yes" it's a "no for now." It's also okay to schedule things for the future rather than feeling pressure to do everything now.

The Power of Flexibility

Life is unpredictable, and you need to be flexible enough to roll with the punches. For example, one minute, you are having the time of your life growing your side business, then the next minute, you are having to withdraw funds from your business to attend to your child's health emergency. Or maybe you have finally built a routine that enables you to have more time for self-care, but with your spouse's new work schedule, they will be less available to help out at home like they used to.

Flexibility is the ability to adjust to unplanned circumstances and continue moving forward. This could mean adopting new routines or strategies to achieve your goals. Ideally, this wouldn't be an option, but since you are being led in a different direction, it's easier to flow with life and work with what you have. The opposite of flexibility is rigidity, which is the inability to adapt to changes, causing you to do things the same way despite receiving new information. Being rigid about your plans gets you stuck in unpleasant situations that seem out of your control to change.

Being flexible starts with your mindset. Ask yourself: Can I rise above this situation or will it overpower me? Your answer will either empower you to look for solutions or find excuses for why you cannot move forward. What you see from your life is what you'll get out of it. Practice making positive assumptions about the unexpected twists and turns that occur in your life. For instance, if work is consuming most of your time and you feel guilty for being away from your kids, try reframing the situation by reminding yourself that you're modeling a strong work ethic and resilience. You can also view this time as an opportunity for your children to develop independence and spend quality time with other caregivers or family members.

If you have found a hobby that sets your heart on fire but you haven't won your partner's approval or support, consider the possibility that they may need time to understand its significance to you. Instead of assuming rejection, think of this as an opportunity for open dialogue, where you can express your passion and invite them to share in your enthusiasm. Their hesitation may stem from unfamiliarity, not disapproval, and with patience and communication, you might gain both their support and a deeper connection. By focusing on the benefits of your inconvenient situation and maintaining a positive outlook, you'll reduce negative emotions and create a more balanced perspective on the challenges you face.

Bonding With Your Family Over Shared Passions

Your interests and passions are meant to be personal activities that allow you to get away from your parenting and spousal duties for a while so you can recharge and reconnect with yourself. But with that said, there are some interests and passions that the whole family can get into and use as a bonding experience. For example, as a family, you might all enjoy traveling, playing sports, trying out new food spots, attending festivals, or watching movies.

Open communication about your shared passion is important to learn more about what each family member enjoys doing. Keep these conversations light and casual in low-stress environments, like during mealtimes or in the car driving somewhere. Take suggestions from your family members as starting points to explore new passions that are brought up.

For example, while browsing social media, one of your older children might show everyone a cool video of a DIY project and suggest that you all try it at home. You can show interest by researching the materials and planning how you would carry it out and what aspects of the project each family member would be responsible for. Eventually, you could complete the project and feel a sense of accomplishment for attempting a new challenge together. One of you may end up taking a serious interest in DIY projects and pursue smaller projects alone.

While sharing passions with your family makes recreational time feel special, ensure that you are spending sufficient time on solo passions that nourish your mind, body, and soul. Remind yourself often that having a life outside your role as a mother or spouse is not selfish. Fundamentally, you are a whole individual with a unique combination of needs that can't all be fulfilled through parenting or your romantic relationships. You need other outlets to help you destress, stimulate your mind, and foster personal growth. Therefore, don't neglect your dreams to raise your family—choose to merge both aspects of your life and find a routine that works best for you!

Chapter 5:

Knowing When to Hit the Pause Button

Almost everything will work again if you unplug it for a few minutes, including you.
—Anne Lamott

The Warning Signs of Being Overwhelmed

Superheroes are invincible men and women children learn about in comics and movies and admire. As natural problem-solvers, they attend to various crises and use their magical powers to save the day—there is no emergency too big for superheroes because they are built for crisis management.

Children often see their parents as real-life superheroes because of their unwavering support, dedication, and selflessness. As explained in the previous chapter, some children may not even realize their parents have needs due to their tendency to put others before themselves. While being held in such high regard by your children can be a wonderful thing, it can also carry negative implications.

Think about it: Superheroes put their lives on hold to respond to cries for help. In the process of helping others, they may experience stress, exhaustion, and physical injuries. Despite everything they go through, they don't have anyone to turn to for support. Since superheroes are immortal beings with unlimited strength, they can afford to continue giving to others without reaching a ceiling. Parents, on the other hand, have a stress and pain threshold, which means that at some point, they need to recharge and take care of themselves to continue giving.

The danger of overextending yourself to your children is that you will eventually feel overwhelmed and experience what is known as parental burnout. This phenomenon occurs whenever parents reach the stage of physical, mental, and emotional exhaustion due to ongoing stress and pressure from their environments. It is recognized by the World Health Organization (WHO) as a work-related syndrome that causes health symptoms ranging from chronic fatigue to changing sleep and diet habits (Abramson, 2021).

Parental burnout is behind some of the conditions you may have that seem unexplainable, such as mood swings, insomnia, hopelessness, or apathy toward your children or parenting duties. Since parenting does come with high pressure, it's normal to feel stressed now and then; however, prolonged stress is a sign to seek help and make necessary changes to your lifestyle. Don't allow the symptoms to fester for too long before you decide to address them. Burnout is a progressive condition that becomes harder to treat with time.

Early Signs to Recognize

If nobody has told you before, please recognize that parenting is a form of work and not an easy one at that. Whether you're a stay-at-home parent or a working parent, the pressures placed on you exceed those of most office jobs. From the time you wake up to the time you finally fall asleep, you are constantly on the go, preempting your children's needs and keeping your household and family life organized.

With the heavy load you are carrying, feeling stressed is inevitable. A decent amount of stress isn't bad for you. In some cases, it could give you the push you need to be productive and get things done. However, severe chronic stress is harmful to your mind and body and needs to be checked to prevent conditions like burnout. Every week, assess your stress levels by reflecting on the areas of your life that are physically and emotionally draining. Journal the symptoms you are noticing and rate them on a scale of 1-10 (1 being light and 10 being extremely severe).

Be extra vigilant for early signs of parental burnout that can appear as:

- feeling tired constantly, even after having sufficient sleep
- struggling to keep up with daily tasks
- finding it hard to enjoy time with your children
- being easily annoyed with minor mistakes your children make
- becoming emotionally withdrawn and distant from your children or partner
- feeling like you aren't doing enough as a parent, doubting your parenting abilities
- daydreaming about your life before you had children and the parenting responsibilities
- neglecting self-care by skipping meals, sleeping late, binging on alcohol, or giving up on your hobbies
- experiencing physical symptoms like chronic migraines, gut issues, and muscle tension

Lifestyle interventions can help you lower and manage stress and treat parental burnout. You don't need medical attention unless you have developed co-occurring conditions like anxiety, suicidal ideation, depression, obsessive-compulsive disorder (OCD), or any other mental health condition. Additionally, psychotherapy is recommended if the burnout is partly caused by ongoing relationship tension, work-life imbalances, or emotional issues that you are having a difficult time processing. Speaking to someone can help you feel supported in your parenting role and prevent feelings of isolation and shame.

Creating Your Own Space: Carving Out Time in a Busy Life

A cost-effective cure for burnout that I highly recommend is getting into the habit of scheduling "me time." This refers to structured or unstructured time spent enjoying your own company, whichever way you like. The amount of "me time" you can have each day or week depends on how busy your schedule is looking. However, even five minutes to check in on yourself is enough to improve your emotional well-being.

Spending time away from your children can often trigger feelings of guilt, especially if you've set the expectation that you must always be available to them. If you find yourself feeling this way, take a moment to reflect on the high standards you've set for yourself and how easily those can lead to feeling overwhelmed. While parenting is undoubtedly a full-time responsibility, it doesn't mean your children need to be by your side every minute of the day. In fact, your children are more resilient than you might realize—they can learn to entertain themselves for 30 minutes or even an hour, giving you the space to recharge without worry.

Instead of seeing "me time" as robbing your children of attention, choose to see it as investing in strengthening your relationship with them. During your moments of solitude, you get to focus on recharging your mind, body, and spirit through relaxing, creative, therapeutic, or playful activities that energize you. Upon returning to your parenting duties, you have more patience and compassion to offer your children since your needs have been taken care of. Being the best parent you can be starts with becoming the best version of yourself, and you can only achieve this through committing to self-care.

Here are four simple ways to become more intentional about scheduling "me time" so you can enjoy guilt-free moments to unwind and fully recharge.

Give Yourself Pep Talks

Pep talks are motivational reminders to believe in yourself. They come in handy whenever you enter spirals of negative thinking and lose sight of how awesome you are. Imagine you had a best friend who was your biggest cheerleader. What would they say to encourage you whenever you need a break? They would probably say, "Go outside for a walk. You'll prepare dinner later." or "Get your nails done. You deserve to treat yourself for getting through this stressful week." In moments of stress and anxiety, talk to yourself like you are your own best friend and stand up for your needs.

Here are some phrases that you can repeat to yourself:
- Caring for myself is not selfish—it's helping me become the best parent I can be.
- My well-being matters because I can't pour from an empty cup.
- I deserve to reward myself for small parenting victories.
- I am not just a parent—I am an individual with needs, dreams, and limits.
- Taking care of myself sends a positive message to my children about self-respect.

Are there any more phrases you can think of? Write them down in your journal and expand the list!

Communicate Your Need for Alone Time

Your family members won't always notice when it's time for you to take a break. This is why communicating your limits and need for alone time is essential. Simply explain that you need to attend to your needs and may be gone for a while. They may want to know details about where you are going and how long you will be. Some children (especially younger ones) could make a fuss about you leaving. To put their minds at ease, let them know your plans at least a few hours before you leave and schedule a fun activity you can play together afterward. It will help them mentally prepare for your brief separation, and they look forward to reuniting later.

Besides your children, you should inform your partner or spouse about your need for alone time. What's great about sharing this need with them is that they can play a supportive role, such as looking after the kids while you're away or taking over some house chores. Most importantly, having this conversation with your partner or spouse allows them inside your inner world so they can validate your emotions and empathize with what you may be going through.

Design a Personal Sanctuary

There will be times when you can't physically leave the house to get some "me time." In these instances, retreating to your sanctuary can feel like taking a vacation while you're inside your home. A personal sanctuary is any space that feels relaxing, nourishing, and completely isolated from the worries of everyday life. This could be your walk-in closet, converted den or backyard shed, cozy garage, or guest bedroom. The functionality of your sanctuary matters more than the size. Here are some elements to consider when designing this space:

- comfortable furniture and accessories like pillows and blankets
- warm-hued LED lighting, including candles, fairy lights, and recessed lighting
- natural lighting to maximize direct sunlight (i.e., draw back the curtains and install big windows)

- declutter the space and invest in multifunctional storage systems
- add soft and personalized touches like your favorite scent or a bright paint color

Browse through home magazines or sites like Pinterest to get inspired by how other people have designed their sanctuaries. Have fun with this project, and remember to celebrate your individuality through every piece of furniture and accessory.

Set Boundaries

One of the most uncomfortable aspects of committing to self-care is having to say no more often. The word "no" is a boundary that protects you from doing more than what's required of you at any given moment. For example, you have to make sure your family has a hot meal for dinner, but you aren't required to cook a meal from scratch every time. Saying "no" to unnecessary pressure allows you to focus on what's truly important—nourishing your family—without sacrificing your own well-being in the process. It's okay to simplify, delegate, or take shortcuts when needed.

Setting boundaries doesn't need to be done using force or threats. Most of the time, your family members will listen and hear you out when you clearly state what you want. Before engaging in this discussion with them, take a moment to consider how you desire to be treated by your children and partner. Think about the behaviors you would like to see more of and those strictly off-limits. Write down your boundaries in clear "I need" statements, such as:

- "I need you to clean up your toys before dinner so we can keep the house organized."
- "I need you to respect your bedtime curfew because rest is important for both of us."
- "I need a few minutes to myself right now, but I'll be available afterward to help you."

Before approaching your family members to discuss your boundaries, imagine how each person will react to the new expectations. For instance, who might be accepting, and who might show resistance? Come up with a plan on how you will maintain your boundaries despite everyone's reactions. This could mean asking your partner to back you up, suggesting a trial period, or walking away from the conversation when it becomes hostile. When sharing your boundaries, offer examples of real-life situations when those boundaries apply, and what actions your family members can take. The simpler it is for them to understand what you need, the easier the adjustment will be.

Finally, strong boundaries come with consequences; these are predictable outcomes that occur whenever your boundaries are violated. Consequences are meant to be teachable moments where you reinforce desirable behaviors. For example, if you have set a rule to have a quiet hour in your house around the same time each day and your child violates that rule, the consequence could be the loss of a privilege, such as screen time or a favorite activity, for that day. This helps them understand that quiet time is important for everyone's well-being and that respecting this boundary leads to a peaceful household while ignoring it has clear and consistent consequences.

Remember that your boundaries are for you, meaning they are designed to lighten the load on your shoulders and make parenting enjoyable. You are allowed to modify your boundaries as your needs and lifestyle change; just be sure to communicate them. Encourage your children to also set boundaries in their own lives so they can prioritize self-care, making it an important value in your family.

Quiz Time: How Well Are You Practicing Self-Care?

To end the chapter, here is a short quiz to help you assess how much you prioritize self-care in your daily life. Go through the multiple-choice questions and answer them truthfully. Then, calculate your score and look at your results.

1. How often do you take time for yourself during the week?

A) Every day

   B) A few times a week

   C) Occasionally

   D) Rarely or never

2. Do you prioritize your physical health (e.g., exercise, nutrition, sleep)?

   A) Always

   B) Most of the time

   C) Sometimes

   D) Hardly ever

3. How do you manage stress on a daily basis?

   A) I have effective stress-relief techniques

   B) I try to manage it, but it's challenging

   C) I occasionally do something to de-stress

   D) I usually just push through it

4. How comfortable are you with asking for help when you need it?

   A) Very comfortable

   B) Somewhat comfortable

   C) I find it difficult

   D) I rarely or never ask for help

5. Do you engage in hobbies or activities that bring you joy?

   A) Regularly

   B) Sometimes

   C) Rarely

   D) Not at all

6. How often do you communicate your needs and feelings with your family?

   A) Frequently and openly

   B) When necessary, but not often

   C) Occasionally, but it's hard

   D) Seldom or never

7. How would you rate your overall work-life balance?

   A) Well-balanced

   B) Somewhat balanced

   C) Struggling to maintain balance

   D) Completely out of balance

Analyze your results:

- **Mostly A's:** You're doing a great job at practicing self-care! Keep it up, and continue to make yourself a priority.
- **Mostly B's:** You're on the right track but could benefit from more consistent self-care practices. Consider adding small, manageable self-care activities to your routine.
- **Mostly C's:** You may be neglecting your own needs. Identify areas in which you can take better care of yourself, even in small ways.
- **Mostly D's:** It's time to focus more on self-care. Your well-being is essential for you and your family. Start with small steps to build healthier habits.

The well-being of your family is intricately linked to your well-being. When you're healthy and emotionally stable, your children flourish. However, when you're overwhelmed and anxious, the entire house gets into disarray. Finding pockets of free time to be alone during the day or practice self-care helps to keep you on your A-Game so that you have more energy to invest in your family relationships. So, why not treat yourself to a movie or catch up with friends? You deserve some time for yourself, and your kids will benefit from having a happier, more refreshed parent!

Chapter 6:

Asking For Help is a Strength, Not a Weakness

To be a good parent, you need to take care of yourself so that you can have the physical and emotional energy to take care of your family. —Michelle Obama

Redefining Strength

There's this cultural belief in our society that "parents should know." This refers to knowing anything and everything about raising their children. Thus, asking for help can be seen as an admission of inadequacy. No parent wants to be looked down upon by their community for seeking advice on how to soothe their baby with colic or discipline their difficult teenager, so they figure it out on their own.

The truth is that perfect parents and children exist on social media and TV shows. In real life, family dynamics are complicated, and children can't be raised with textbook knowledge alone. Families are made up of real people with real thoughts and feelings. Managing every family member's needs, attitudes, mindsets, and temperaments isn't a job that Mom or Dad can do on their own. They need support from a reliable network of friends, family, and professionals who can weigh in on some problems and offer emotional support, physical support, expert advice, or counseling.

To make asking for help "cool," we can work toward redefining what strength means. The simple definition of strength is the quality of being strong or displaying power (Merriam-Webster, 2019). In our society, strength or power is commonly associated with traditional masculine qualities such as:

- **Physical power:** The ability to perform strenuous or demanding physical tasks.
- **Emotional resilience:** Staying composed and managing intense emotions under pressure.
- **Leadership:** The power to take charge, make decisions, and guide others through challenging situations.
- **Stoicism:** The ability to endure hardship without showing visible signs of distress or vulnerability.
- **Self-reliance:** The capacity to handle problems independently, depending on your skillsets, knowledge, and experience.

Looking at these qualities, we can see why parents might be opposed to asking for help—it goes against the definition of what it means to be strong. Redefining strength for ourselves as parents allows us to reclaim our power to choose how we raise our children. Strength doesn't need to be viewed as being invincible, self-sufficient, and always in control. It could be viewed as the ability to adapt to change, collaborate with other parents, offer compassion, and recognize your own limitations.

Indeed, strong parents are resilient; however, their resilience doesn't isolate them. It makes them aware of their need for others and humble enough to ask for assistance. Strong parents know that parenting children has its ups and downs, so nurturing relationships with other parents and professionals ensures that there is a community of supporters they can rely on for encouragement. They recognize that collaborative efforts lead to better outcomes than going through it alone.

How to Master Delegation

The first step to asking for help is recognizing that you need it. Start by reviewing your to-do list or daily schedule, taking note of the tasks and responsibilities you're juggling. If you're someone who doesn't usually write things down, now is a great time to list your daily activities to get a clear picture of how your time is spent. Once you've taken stock, ask yourself whether you're managing well. Do you feel like you're staying afloat, or are you overwhelmed and sinking under the weight of it all? This reflection can help you identify where help is needed.

For example, a typical working mother balances work duties and parenting duties. On some days, she might come back from work feeling tired and not prepared to complete the long list of chores she had written down. Other times, she might feel emotionally overspent and can't help her children with their homework. Two areas where she could benefit from support are handling house chores and getting her children on a routine so they are less reliant on her involvement, particularly during weekdays.

Once you are aware of your need for help, the next step is to ask for it. Most times, parents ask for help as a one-time request, which can alleviate stress for that day but doesn't provide a long-term solution. The better approach is to delegate tasks to family members, which they take on as their new responsibilities. Using the example made above, the working mother could delegate some house chores like tidying the living room, folding laundry, preparing dinners for her children, and distributing tasks according to their age and capabilities. Additionally, she could design a structured after-school homework and bedtime routine for each child that promotes greater independence.

Delegating tasks is about lessening the load for the most burdened family member so everyone gets involved in running the home and keeping the family healthy and functional. With that said, there are some do's and don'ts for effective delegation that you should remember, such as:

Start Small

When preparing to delegate tasks, try not to overwhelm your family members with huge responsibilities. Start small by assigning manageable tasks that they can easily accomplish. For example, it should be tasks that don't require many steps to complete or advanced skills or techniques. You can teach your children how to perform more intricate tasks with time and practice. By then, they would have built more confidence in themselves to make the tasks feel less daunting.

Choose the Right Individual for Each Task

Think about which family member would be suited for each task and how things such as their interests, stress tolerance, and personality can influence their success in completing the task. For example, an energetic 13-year-old won't be the best person for a detail-oriented and slow task like washing dishes; instead, they might enjoy and be good at sorting laundry or vacuuming the house. It's also important to take into consideration your children's preferences when delegating tasks. Present two options and let them choose the one they prefer.

Communicate Instructions Clearly

When your children have been given a task to do, the last thing they want is to disappoint you. They may not show it, but deep down they desire to impress you and receive validation. Therefore, to help your children succeed, give them clear and actionable instructions to follow. Use multiple formats to display the instructions to accommodate each child's learning style. For example, you could:

- write the instructions on paper
- vocalize the instruction in a respectful tone
- add the task to your child's calendar
- place colorful reminders around the house
- draw a diagram or flow chart to illustrate the process
- leave a physical demonstration that they can look at and follow

Avoid making commands when delegating tasks, as this makes your children feel forced rather than motivated to complete them. As they get older and can think for themselves, they may become defensive whenever you command them to do something. Remember that respect is not given; it's earned. How you communicate with your children is how they will later communicate with you.

Be respectful of their time, needs, and feelings when making your requests, imagining yourself being on the receiving end. If your child refuses to complete a task, have a conversation about it and find out what they are having trouble with. Come up with a solution that satisfies both of you while ensuring the task is accomplished. This could mean being open to your child completing the task using their own creative methods.

Offer Constructive Feedback

Once again, your children desire to please you when you have asked them to help you with tasks. Be extra sensitive to their feelings whenever giving feedback on the completed job. Remind yourself that they aren't an expert at cleaning, cooking, ironing, or decluttering and will need positive reinforcement to improve their skills and achieve the standard that you've set. Circling back to the subject of individuality, remind yourself that each person carries out tasks in their own way. Common sense doesn't apply here since everyone has their own mental processing models.

For instance, when cooking, you might start by preparing your ingredients and laying them on the counter in the exact measurements.

Your older child might have a spontaneous approach, choosing to take out ingredients as and when they are mentioned in the recipe. You might also clean as you go to prevent a pile-up of dishes, but your child might complete a clean-up at the end. Instead of criticizing them for their system, accept that there's more than one way of cooking, but the ultimate goal is to prepare delicious meals.

If your child has made mistakes that you seek to correct, use the sandwich feedback technique to communicate what they did well and what they can improve next time. This involves starting and ending with praise whenever you are suggesting areas of improvement. For example, picture your older child preparing mac-and-cheese for the first time, and they mistakenly add too much salt. Here's how you would provide constructive feedback using the sandwich technique (Kostiana, 2023):

- **Start with praise:** "I'm really proud of you for making dinner on your own—it's great that you're learning to cook and taking responsibility!"
- **Suggest area of improvement:** "Next time, try adding a little less salt. You can always add more later if needed, but it's harder to fix once there's too much."
- **End with praise:** "Overall, you did an awesome job! With just a bit of practice, you're going to be a fantastic cook. Keep it up, and I can't wait to try your next dish!"

Practice this simple technique by yourself using common examples of your children making fixable mistakes when completing tasks. Be mindful of your tone of voice and approach when giving feedback.

Finding the Right Help, Professional or Personal

"It takes a village to raise a child"—this African proverb emphasizes the need for community-centric parenting to raise children into well-adjusted and responsible adults (Hinds, 2020). Think of back in the day when communities were more integrated than they are today. Grandparents, aunts, uncles, and even neighbors would become surrogate parents. In their loving care, children would be fed, nurtured, and disciplined, just like they would be at home.

Of course, times have changed, and communities are less interconnected than before. However, that doesn't mean you cannot build your own community of supporters. It may not be your friends, family members, or neighbors; sometimes your greatest supporters aren't people you grew up with but rather people you've met online, at parent meetings, on forums, and other communal spaces.

Find Your Tribe

Every parent needs a tribe of supporters available to offer different types of support. Some people might be great encourages; others might provide expert knowledge. The absence of support makes parenting feel lonely and demanding. Instead of having someone to vent to or share the parenting load with, you can only depend on yourself.

Your tribe should consist of people whose values and beliefs align with yours, people who are going in the same direction as you and desire similar goals. There's no use in connecting with people whose parenting approach and lifestyle contradict yours. Initially, you might learn something new from them, but in the long run, your needs and expectations may clash.

When looking for members of your tribe, start by creating a list of the areas of parenting that you need support with. For example, you might need support to navigate your pregnancy journey, create structure and routines once your child is born, or manage parenting duties as your child grows up. For each item, identify someone you know or a professional who can assist you in that area. Maybe you have some close friends who are parents or family members whose parenting approach you admire.

There could also be professionals who are medical doctors or holistic healers whose methods you resonate with. They can help you find a parenting style that aligns with your needs and interests. After identifying these people, contact them and request that they join your tribe. Look for ways to make your relationship mutually beneficial, such as finding ways that you can support them on their parenting journeys or professional practices.

Maintaining a strong and responsive tribe in the long term can be difficult because life happens and sometimes you or the people you depend on may not be available. In cases like these, patience and compassion for yourself and members of your tribe is essential. Find alternative ways to stay in touch if physically meeting isn't possible and reassure each other in small ways of your support.

How to Ask for Support

After identifying people who could be part of your support system, the next step is communicating the specific role you envision them playing in your life. Be clear about the type of support you'll need and ask if they're willing and able to provide it and how frequently. Not everyone will be the right person to turn to for emotional support, as some may excel in offering practical advice or providing hands-on help when needed. Understanding and respecting each person's strengths can create a more balanced and effective support network.

Believe it or not, there's also a method to asking for support. It's not as simple as making a request and waiting for a yes or no answer. Here are some valuable points to consider before you ask for support:

- **Inspire others to help you by being supportive.** When you are helpful to others, it fosters a sense of mutual support and encourages them to be more eager to help you in return. To strengthen your relationships and inspire your supporters to enthusiastically address your needs, make it a priority to be available when they need assistance. Often, they won't even have to ask—when you notice an opportunity to help, be proactive and offer your support to demonstrate that you are a reliable person.
- **Be specific about what you need.** Getting supporters on board is easier when they clearly know what you need from them. Is it borrowing money? If so, how much, how can they send it, and when can they expect to get it back? Provide as much

information as required to help them make their decision and see where their support is needed.

- **Find the right person to ask.** Once again, not everyone is qualified to offer every type of support. In general, there are three types of support—practical, emotional, and informational—that address different needs. Practical support involves physically solving a problem by getting involved. Emotional support offers encouragement to get through a difficult time. Informational support equips you with knowledge to help solve problems. These types of support can rarely be offered by the same person.

- **Give the other person an option to decline.** Even though you may be desperate when asking for help, you cannot force others to attend to your emergencies; you can only request their support and allow them to accept or decline, based on their capacity and willingness. Anticipate the possibility of rejection and come up with a viable Plan B that you can try. Remind yourself that rejection is not a personal attack on your character and shouldn't make you feel bad.

If you are somebody who dislikes asking for support because of how vulnerable it makes you feel, try rehearsing how you would ask for support in front of a mirror. Practice what you would say and how you would respond to different questions. You can also rehearse the worst-case scenarios, such as being turned down, to mentally prepare yourself for all possibilities. Your fear of rejection shouldn't be a barrier that stops you from seeking the help you need.

Asking for help isn't something that society views as a strength. However, by redefining the meaning of strength, you can associate asking for help with courage, humility, and collaboration. True strength comes from recognizing that you need help and permitting yourself to seek it. It takes a village to raise a child, so who are your supporters, and how can you reach out to them today?

Chapter 7:

Redefining What Success Means in Parenting

Parenting is about raising and celebrating the child you have, not the child you thought you'd have. –Brene Brown

Embracing the Growth Mindset

Your self-evaluation as a parent matters more than what others think of you. This is because your thoughts shape your emotions, attitudes, and behaviors. Think about how harmful a statement like "I have failed as a parent" can be to your psyche when rehearsed many times. Eventually, your everyday circumstances will reflect the failure that you have visualized in your mind. Even moments of pure bliss with your children will be overshadowed by internal feelings of regret and shame.

Controlling your thoughts begins with intentionally shifting your mindset by transforming your beliefs, assumptions, and internal dialogue. While it may sound cliché, positive and empowering thoughts truly have the potential to reshape your life. A helpful analogy is to think of your mind as a garden and your thoughts as seeds. You have the power to choose which seeds to plant, but remember that not all seeds grow into fragrant flowers and nourishing fruits—some will grow into weeds. It's up to you to nurture the thoughts that help you flourish and weed out the ones that hinder your growth.

The author of the best-selling book *Mindset*, Carol Dweck, describes two common types of mindsets that can positively or negatively impact your outlook on life (Dweck, 2019). The first is a fixed mindset that places restrictions on what you can and cannot achieve based on current skills, knowledge, and experience. It is motivated by the fear of the unknown and the perceived safety of your comfort zone. In contrast, the second mindset is known as the growth mindset, which promotes an expansive view of life and the possibilities about who you can become. Your current skills, knowledge, and experience are seen as a starting point rather than the end, and your setbacks are viewed as feedback rather than failure.

Pause from reading and reflect on what type of mindset you currently have. Do you lean more toward a fixed or growth mindset? Are you driven by the fears or opportunities that come with parenting? Note that it's possible to embrace a growth mindset in some areas but not others. For example, you might encourage your children to express their unique identities and pursue their interests and hobbies, but on the other hand, you might still use outdated forms of traditional discipline that impede their self-expression.

Or maybe you motivate your children to achieve academic success because the process of learning teaches them commitment and dedication. However, at home, you are reluctant to assign your children small responsibilities like completing house chores, which would reinforce those same values. What we can all learn from these examples is that embracing a growth mindset is not easy, but it isn't impossible either. Below are suggestions of habits that can help you apply a growth mindset to all areas of parenting and strengthen your relationship with your children.

Find Purpose in Failure

Can you recall how failure was introduced to you as a child? Did you grow up in an environment that encouraged you to learn from your mistakes? The reality is that how you introduce the concept of failure to your children can influence their willingness or reluctance to accept challenges.

Teach your children that a failure is an event that isn't attached to their character, meaning they can fail without labeling themselves as failures. Moreover, the event can be interpreted in two ways: either as a lesson learned or a reminder of inherent weaknesses. Help your children see the hidden value of failure: It provides necessary feedback to help them refine their goals and emerge stronger than before. Provide examples from their past experiences of times when failure turned out to be beneficial.

As a parent, you can also reflect on times when your parenting mistakes were opportunities to learn something new or seek support. Your failures as a parent do not make you more or less competent to raise your children. You are already an exceptional parent; failures simply help you level up and enhance your skills.

Allow Your Children to Dream

One of the magical experiences of childhood is tapping into your imagination and envisioning a future without the limitations of real-life circumstances. During these creative moments, children follow their curiosity and imagine the person they can become, which can inspire them to develop new interests.

Allowing your children the space to dream means creating an environment at home that supports their potential. This could mean purchasing toys and books related to their interests or scheduling unstructured "free time" every day where your children can engage in creative pursuits. Celebrating your children's potential could also be something you instill through goal setting. For instance, you could sit together and collaborate on setting short-term goals, then have regular check-ins to provide feedback on their progress. Whenever they reach a milestone, celebrate their progress and reflect on how far they have come.

Bear in mind that it's easier to accept your children's dreams when you are working toward achieving your own. If you have dreams that you have placed on hold, now is the time to revisit them and find ways to integrate them into your lifestyle. You don't have to make big commitments all at once; even a small action that you can perform daily is enough to start the momentum and reignite your fire (refer to Chapter 4).

Focus on Principles, Not Perfection

Your children will make mistakes and do things to upset you. When correcting them, emphasize the principle they have overlooked rather than the behavior that they couldn't get right. Focusing on principles allows your children to take the lessons from one situation and transfer them to another similar situation because principles don't change. However, when you make a big deal about their behavior, they change their actions without understanding the far-reaching impact of them.

An example is a teenager who needs to be repeatedly reminded to do their homework. Every day, they forget about their homework and choose to spend that time playing video games instead. The only time they get up is when their mother pleads with them. What can they learn from their mother's constant reminders? The truth is nothing. However, when their mother decides to explain the principles of hard work, commitment, and accountability behind doing homework, the child suddenly understands the impact of not doing their homework. They can see they are learning a bad habit that can jeopardize their schooling career and future.

To reinforce these principles, their mother could step back and resist the urge to remind them about their homework every day, instead allowing them to take full responsibility and experience the natural consequences of their choices. Some children need uncomfortable wake-up calls—like failing a test or receiving a negative behavior report—to truly grasp the importance of the values their parents are trying to instill. The goal isn't to punish them but to help them understand that the same principles guiding their success at home also apply to other areas of life, teaching them accountability and self-discipline.

Provide Growth-Oriented Feedback

Growth-oriented feedback is designed to help your children bounce back from setbacks, using words that allow them to see themselves as strong and capable people. Two techniques are important to remember when providing growth-oriented feedback. The first is to praise the process rather than praising the child. For instance, instead of saying, "You are so smart!" which can be true for this moment but may not be true in another situation, you can say, "I can see you've improved; keep up the good work!" The person's character is fixed, but the process is an ever-changing journey that makes room for failure and growth. Praising the process helps your children see their tangible progress and feel competent.

The second technique is to offer process-related praise rather than vague praise. If you are wondering what vague praise sounds like, here are some examples:

- "Nice job!"
- "Well done!"
- "You're the best!"
- "I'm proud of you!"
- "That was awesome!"

The trouble with vague praise is that your children don't have something tangible to feel proud of or to benchmark their progress. They are told that they are good, but for doing what exactly? Process-related praise explains what your child has done to warrant the recognition so that next time, they are aware of what they need to do to get the same results or reaction from you. Here are some examples of process-related praise:

- "I'm proud of how hard you worked on that project, even when it got challenging."
- "I noticed how focused you were while practicing; that kind of dedication will really pay off."
- "It's impressive how you didn't give up when you got stuck on that math problem, and you figured it out!"
- "I love how you took your time and didn't rush through this. Your careful approach made a big difference."
- "The way you're breaking this down into smaller tasks shows you're thinking strategically."

Sometimes, as a parent, you need to give yourself the same kind of process-related praise to remind yourself of your positive impact on your children's lives. At least once a day, before you go to bed, look at yourself in the mirror and recall one thing you did well that day that you are proud of. For instance, it could be:

- "I've been really patient today, even when things got tough. That's progress."
- "I kept showing up, even when it was exhausting—that kind of persistence matters."
- "I tried different approaches to connect with my kids, and that effort is helping us grow."
- "I made time for self-care today, and that's a step toward better balance."
- "I handled that tantrum well by staying present and listening—my effort to improve is paying off."

Affirm Your Parenting Reality

Your parenting journey won't feel completely satisfying as long as you seek validation from others to affirm that you are an awesome parent. This doesn't mean that you shouldn't take compliments or listen to constructive criticism when it's given; however, don't hold the feedback you get from other people in such a high regard that it defines who you are. Everyone has opinions, but that's all they are—opinions. You know the everyday experiences of raising your children and what they truly need to succeed.

To drown out the external noise from good-intentioned friends, family, neighbors, and social media critics, learn to affirm yourself with positive self-talk. Self-validation is about acknowledging and showing compassion toward your thoughts, feelings, and experiences, even when you aren't necessarily proud of your actions. It is the epitome of self-love because you extend unconditional love and kindness to yourself, whether you believe you deserve it or not.

Self-validation can also strengthen self-belief, making it easier for you to trust your parenting choices. Since you know all of this information about yourself, such as how you handle stress, what areas of discipline you struggle with, or what makes you feel fulfilled as a parent, you can start making decisions that are aligned with your values, vision, and needs rather than what's socially acceptable. Ultimately, through self-validation, you become an independent thinker who can scrutinize ideas and advice that come from the world and draw conclusions based on your inner wisdom.

Self-validating takes time, especially when you have been accustomed to following trends and seeking approval from others. However, it's a skill that can be learned by following these useful tips:

Don't Deny How You Feel

Be aware of your emotions without pushing them away. Realize that sometimes, you'll be tempted to suppress, numb, or downplay your emotions to avoid the pain and get through the day. However, this can quickly turn into a pattern of dissociating from unpleasant emotions. If you need to temporarily push your emotions to the side, schedule time later that day to revisit those feelings and listen to yourself. In the privacy of your bedroom or bathroom, give yourself the opportunity to feel whatever emotions you have denied during the day and release them. You can cry, scream, sing, or talk to yourself—whatever you need to allow the emotions to pass through and out of your body.

See Things As They Are, Not As You Wish Them to Be

Another form of dissociating is attaching yourself to a made-up reality of parenting and raising your children that exists in your head but never quite translates into reality. Maybe this idea was influenced by images and videos you saw on social media or movies that you have watched. During stressful times, fantasizing about this made-up reality could be your short-term coping mechanism; you feel good about your life for a few minutes until you realize you are daydreaming. Seeing your life as it is may not always be encouraging because, like other parents, you go through hardships with your family. The benefit, however, is that by accepting your reality, you learn to cope with real-life stressors and find a way to make the most of your parenting journey despite them.

Validate Your Fears

You are not wrong or dramatic to feel afraid, insecure, or anxious about your parenting journey. These emotions surface because they are in some way linked to past experiences where you faced similar realities. For example, your fear of letting someone else watch your baby for you could stem from childhood experiences where you or someone you know was hurt by someone responsible for watching them. Your insecurity around your ability to raise your children could stem from past situations when you felt criticized by others for your life choices. Instead of judging your fears, recognize where they come from and validate why you would still feel this way. Repeat affirming statements to yourself like, "It makes sense for me to feel afraid of confronting my teenager because when I was a child, my parents would say hurtful words during arguments."

Normalize Not Being Happy All the Time

Ideally, parenting is supposed to be this transformative experience that helps you become a better version of yourself. While this does happen, it won't be your everyday experience. The harsh reality is that you won't feel happy all the time or have victories to celebrate. Some days, weeks, or months could feel boring, lonely, or demanding. At the same time, it's important to remind yourself that you are not the only parent in the world who is having a difficult time. Many mothers and fathers across racial, cultural, and geographical borders can relate to what you are going through. You can engage with some of them by joining parenting forums or social media groups and talking openly about your circumstances. You'll see from the flood of responses that your thoughts and emotions are normal, and there are solutions.

Celebrate the Small Wins: Find Joy in the Everyday

Unless you deliberately look for moments to appreciate your parenting journey, you won't find many reasons to celebrate. Even though a single day feels long, the years of parenting go by very quickly, and before you know it the child you were breastfeeding is going to daycare, and the teenager whose attitude gave you headaches is now going to college.

Gratitude is the quality of being thankful for the small or big moments of your life. This kind of attitude and awareness requires you to focus on what is going well rather than what you are struggling with. We know that parenting isn't perfect and that there will be times when you want to hide out in your bedroom, away from your children. In those moments of stress, intentionally shifting your focus to what you are grateful for can help you calm down and regain perspective.

Celebrating the small wins of parenting is exactly what it sounds like—taking moments to pause and appreciate your parenting milestones or simply reflecting on how far you've come. You don't always need to do something exceptional to celebrate your parenting journey. You can express gratitude for small things like dropping your kids at school on time or noticing when you are triggered and stepping aside to breathe and recollect yourself.

Your mindset also plays a role in helping you recognize moments worth celebrating. For instance, if you have a fixed mindset, you are more likely to celebrate perfect outcomes and downplay the efforts you've made to change your behaviors or learn new skills. Moreover, you might only allow yourself to pursue things you are truly good at and, therefore, miss out on opportunities to appreciate the small steps toward becoming a better parent.

However, with a growth mindset, any progress is worthy of recognition because you are more committed to your process of personal transformation rather than being a perfect parent. This mindset allows you to be less critical of your performance since every victory or loss can be used as valuable feedback to improve your efforts. Therefore, whether you have had a good or bad day, you celebrate the fact that you are heading in the right direction, proactively building the dream life you desire for your family.

There aren't any hard rules about how you can practice gratitude. However, here are some suggestions for daily habits you can adopt that remind you of the incredible responsibility you have of being a parent and the amazing strides you are making:

- Create a "Ta-da" list to recognize the small victories throughout each day. Don't think too hard about what to put on your list. It could be any task, thought, emotion, or behavior that makes you feel like "I've got this!"

- Schedule time for daily reflection. So much happens throughout the day, especially when you have a busy schedule. Find a quiet moment toward the end of the day to reflect on what you accomplished, the problems you solved, or anything that brought a smile to your face.

- Be excitable about trivial things. Train your mind to get a dopamine release from trivial things that happen during the day, such as getting an email response you were waiting for, hearing a funny joke, or having silly moments with your children. These moments remind you that life doesn't always need to be serious.

- Share your good news with someone. Whenever you get good news or achieve a personal victory, find someone to share it with. It's not about bragging to your friends and family but allowing them to celebrate with you and acknowledge your progress.
- Reward yourself with tangible gifts. Some wins, like successfully potty-training your child or getting through a rough patch with one of your older children, warrant gifting. You deserve to treat yourself to a day of spoils to recognize the physical, mental, and emotional labor you have put in to get to where you are. Create a personal gifting list you can refer to every time you want to congratulate yourself.

Gratitude is a strength that isn't always recognized as one. The ability to shift your focus from negative to positive thoughts can alter your mood, choices, and behaviors and help you dig yourself out of parenting ruts that are so common. In the long term, your ability to succeed at parenting rests on the quality of your mindset. What you focus on in your mind becomes what you see taking shape in your real life. Practice choosing how you desire to feel and get through each moment of the day because, truly, the power to improve your parenting experience lies with you!

Chapter 8:

The Ripple Effect: Long-Term Benefits of Prioritizing Yourself

You cannot pour from an empty cup. Take care of yourself first. —Eleanor Roosevelt

The Connection Between Self-Care and Resilience

Throughout the book, taking care of yourself has been a recurring theme. Many parenting books focus on the well-being of children and what they need to feel fulfilled. However, this book has emphasized the importance of your well-being in raising healthy and happy children. After all, when you're not in a good mental and emotional space, how effective can you be at responding to your children's needs?

In the long term, self-care will transform your relationship with yourself and strengthen the relationships with your children and partner. In particular, long-term self-care leads to resilience, which is the ability to self-regulate and bounce back from setbacks. You'll notice that your family members are less dependent on you for their emotional regulation because watching you practice self-care models to them how they should be managing stress and anxiety.

Imagine your household is a military training camp where your children learn how to respond to life's difficulties. Granted, this training ground has some comforts that the world won't give them freely, but it's also a place where they learn vital life lessons. As the military generals, you and your spouse or partner have the enormous responsibility of training these young soldiers to succeed in life. Under your guidance, they learn to carry themselves by following house rules and mimicking your behaviors.

When you practice self-care, you remind your children to prioritize their needs above anything else. For instance, when they are hungry, they learn to prepare meals for themselves and eat rather than wait for you to hand them a plate or for their hunger pangs to hit. When they are feeling down, they learn to turn to healthy outlets like journaling or listening to music to process their emotions. These positive coping strategies they adopt are learned through observing how you navigate everyday circumstances and prioritize your needs. So, self-care isn't selfish but one of the underrated techniques for instilling confidence and resilience in your children.

Encouraging Independence Through Self-Care

Another benefit of practicing self-care is that you get to encourage your children to become more independent. This doesn't mean letting them do everything themselves but instead allowing them to take care of needs that they are capable of responding to on their own while being on standby to assist them.

Independence offers your children a sense of freedom to make decisions concerning their lives. Of course, they may not always make the right decisions; however, being able to choose what they will wear, eat, watch, or do on the weekends increases their sense of self-worth. Independence is also what empowers your children to feel a greater sense of control during difficult moments or transitional periods in their lives.

You may have a small child who's strongly attached to you and needs your help to complete basic tasks like feeding themselves or putting on clothes. Or a teenager who relies on you to remind them of their daily tasks, pick up after them, or solve their problems. Being there for your child 24/7 is appropriate when they are infants because they need you for survival. However, after a child reaches a certain age (between 3-5) and hasn't been diagnosed with any developmental or neurological disorder, then it's expected for them to show some agency in taking care of their basic needs.

Encouraging independence won't cause an emotional disconnect between you and your child. If anything, it can enhance your connection by enabling them to gain confidence and be responsible for their own happiness. Their independence can also free up more of your time during the day, which you can allocate to pursuing your interests and hobbies. In the end, both of you feel deeply satisfied in your relationship.

Bear in mind that not all children like the idea of doing things by themselves. Some may resist the idea and throw tantrums whenever they are asked to perform tasks independently, while others might love the autonomy. Below are several tips that you can try to encourage independence. Introduce them gradually to your children and see how they react. If they respond well, continue practicing them, but if not, try something else.

Offer Choices

To test the waters, especially with young children, offer two choices whenever presenting tasks and allow them to choose their preferred option. For example, when you're preparing dinner and need to distract your little one with an activity, you could say, "What would you like to do while I cook dinner: draw a picture or play with Legos?" For an older child, you might offer choices when allowing them to pick their house chores. You could say, "Okay buddy, this week you have the option of cleaning up after dinner or changing the rubbish bags. What's your pick?" Presenting choices gives your children a sense of ownership of their actions and makes them feel like their opinions matter.

Encourage Healthy Risk-Taking

Whenever possible, encourage your children to do things that fall outside their comfort zones, as long as they won't hurt themselves or others. Healthy risk-taking builds social and emotional intelligence. The possibility of failure is necessary to teach them how to set goals and navigate challenges creatively. Examples of healthy risk-taking include joining a sports team, entering a debate competition, making new friends, or standing up for themselves in public. These risks can increase your children's self-confidence and show them what they are capable of achieving when they believe in themselves.

Lead From Behind

Your children may never reach their full potential if you're always walking in front of them. They need the opportunity to lead, discovering their talents and strengths along the way. Leading from behind means creating clear boundaries while stepping back, allowing your children to decide how they operate within those limits. While you can offer guidance when needed, it's essential to let them explore the world on their own terms.

For example, you might set the expectation that homework is completed before dinner. Whether they choose to do it right after school or 30 minutes beforehand is entirely up to them. Another example is allowing your older child to go out with friends, trusting that they will act responsibly. Instead of checking in every 20 minutes, you might ask them to contact you only if there's an emergency. This approach fosters trust, independence, and accountability, helping them learn to navigate life with confidence.

Pick Your Battles

Ongoing tension and conflict in your parent-child relationships can be draining and turn the atmosphere at home sour. To maintain harmony, learn to pick your battles with your children. Not every disagreement warrants extreme measures. Sometimes, negotiating, walking away, or pretending like you didn't hear the rude comment can be a form of self-care. This is because you avoid the negative energies that would bring you down. If possible, you might even allow your child to make the final decision on matters related to entertainment or scheduling. However, anything that has to do with their health, safety, and future prospects needs to be discussed formally, and you have the final say.

Creating a Healthy Family Dynamic

Parenting is not supposed to be a debate with your children, but you do need to be on the same page about what kind of home environment you desire to create. If you haven't done this before, bring your children together and answer this simple question as a family: *What does a healthy and balanced family look like for us?*

The answer to this question will be different for every family, which is the point. There are no two families that are the same. What your family needs to feel fulfilled might not look the same as what another family finds fulfilling. This is also why open discussions with your children about this topic are essential when deciding the dynamic you want to create at home. Their input can help you collaborate on establishing a culture representing the values that matter most to all of you.

Collaborating to form a healthy family dynamic ensures your family life is structured and predictable. Your family members know what roles they play and how they can build and nurture relationships with other members of the household. Moreover, everyone feels empowered to voice their opinions and share ideas to make the family better. During your brainstorming sessions, consider the qualities that make families strong and resilient. Here are some questions you can also think about:

- What does your family enjoy doing for fun?
- Does your family have rules, and are they followed?
- What reasonable expectations do you have of each other?
- How do parents and children treat each other in your family?
- How does your family deal with conflict and stress?
- How does your family express love and support to one another?

The foundation of your family dynamic is built on your values; these are principles that your family lives by. Defining your values can do two things: it can set healthy standards for your family members to aim toward while also making each family member responsible for their actions. This means that even when you are not watching, your children are reminded of how they should approach various situations and can modify their behaviors accordingly.

Similar to the discussion about your family dynamic, you must have an open conversation about your family values. Older children can even help you write up a list of your values on a poster that you can hang somewhere visible in the house. When reflecting on your values, think about the following:

- What do we want our family to be known for?
- How do we prioritize self-care and mental health?
- What's important to us when it comes to work, education, and pursuing goals?
- What role does community play in our family life?
- What makes us feel connected as a family?
- How do we want to treat each other during disagreements?

Narrow down your list to 5-7 values, then create a mission statement about a paragraph long that represents what your family values and stands for. Start your statement with "we as the [Last Name] family..." to display a sense of unity and pride.

Celebrating the Ripple Effect

Your continued efforts to prioritize your own needs will create a powerful ripple effect, allowing you to positively influence your children without imposing any behaviors on them. They will naturally feel inspired to become the best version of themselves in all areas of their lives. Many parents spend thousands on therapists trying to shape their children's mindset, but no amount of money can override someone's free will. Real transformation only occurs when children decide for themselves to make a change. The secret to influencing your children, without cost, is focusing on becoming the best version of yourself as a parent. With that in mind, here are some valuable tips to help you achieve this:

Be Available for Yourself

Nothing truly says "My well-being matters" than spending time responding to your needs and doing the things you love. In between your parenting duties, don't neglect your basic needs like eating, sleeping, taking a shower, and drinking hot coffee! Remember that it's okay to have bad days where you are less available for others. Delegate tasks you cannot manage and be clear about the support you need.

Listen, But Don't Be Quick to Fix

Fixing things is one of your superpowers as a parent, but sometimes the more you fix, the more trouble you cause in the long run. Your children need to learn how to apply their minds to solving the problems they face. This is a crucial life skill that needs to be fully developed by the time they leave home. Be there to provide emotional support and validate what they are going through. If they ask for help, feel free to offer advice, but ultimately reassure them that they are capable of finding solutions.

Stand Up for Yourself

Children learn the difference between right and wrong behavior by testing your boundaries and watching how you react. When they misbehave, and you don't show any resistance, you are teaching them that it's okay to mistreat others or to be mistreated. Standing up for yourself is a display of self-respect, courage, and assertiveness. It could be standing up to your child when they throw an object at you or standing up to your spouse when they embarrass you in public. The message you send across is clear: "No means no." Even if your child or spouse doesn't like being called out, they learn to honor your limits.

Don't Be a Buzz Kill

Parenting doesn't always need to be strategic. Sometimes, the best way to influence your children is by having fun with them. Playfulness connects to the heart of your children and fosters a deeper understanding of who they are and what they care about. During fun activities, they are also more open, curious, and relaxed, which makes engaging in meaningful conversations a lot easier. Don't let a day go by without laughing together or sharing playful moments like wrestling, cuddling, cooking a recipe, or singing karaoke.

Express Gratitude

How often do you thank your children for the contributions they make around the house or the efforts they put into improving their behavior? Saying "thank you" shows that you recognize something positive in your child and want them to know it. When they hear those words, it gives them a chance to reflect on their strengths and feel appreciated. Over time, they begin to associate the feeling of pride with the gratitude you express, fostering a deeper connection with you for making them feel valued. This acknowledgment can inspire them to continue striving for positive behaviors, motivated by the simple but powerful words "thank you."

These are certainly not all the ways that you can become a better parent, but at least a starting point. As you continue working on yourself, you will spontaneously discover and adopt other habits that increase the influence you have on your children. The aim is to follow your authentic parenting path and align with practices that make you feel confident about yourself.

You will never regret prioritizing yourself because it's the best investment you can make in improving your family life. Putting your needs first reminds your children of the importance of self-care. They learn that it's not your responsibility to make them happy but an inside job they can do on their own. In the long term, you can collectively establish a positive culture of compassion in your family where you are considerate of each other's needs and work as a team to solve problems.

Conclusion:

Embracing the Journey Ahead with Grace

Being a parent can be tough. But just remember that in your child's eyes, nobody does it better than you. –Unknown

Parenting is a journey full of ups and downs, and no matter how many kids you have—one or several—it will always look different than anyone else's experience. Each child you raise is going to bring something new to the table. You might find yourself swapping stories with friends or relatives, finding common ground in sleepless nights, or dealing with tantrums, but the truth is, your parenting journey will always be unique.

It's important to remember that while children learn from everything around them, they are also their own people. They will push boundaries, test your patience, and often remind you of the person you were when you were their age. This is part of what makes raising kids so special—they force you to grow and reflect on your own life, often in ways you didn't expect. They aren't just sponges soaking up everything you teach them; they are constantly learning, exploring, and developing their own personalities.

Don't fall into the trap of feeling like you need to be in control all the time. Let your kids see you handle things as they come. Whether you're dealing with a meltdown or celebrating a small victory, it's all part of the parenting journey. The truth is, none of us have it all figured out, and that's okay. What matters is being present and embracing the reality that every family is different, and every moment with your child is an opportunity to connect and grow together.

Instead of trying to keep everything perfect, lean into the chaos. Yes, parenting can be exhausting and overwhelming at times, but it's also full of moments you'll look back on and treasure. Spilled milk, toys scattered everywhere, impromptu pillow fights—all of it is part of the experience. Kids grow up fast, and the last thing you want is to realize you rushed through the good parts, trying to keep everything tidy.

So, give yourself some grace. Mistakes will happen, and that's fine—just keep learning as you go. Appreciate your child's individuality, celebrate the highs and lows, and remember there's no one-size-fits-all approach to parenting. Most importantly, don't miss out on the special moments by getting caught up in trying to do everything perfectly. These years are fleeting; before you know it, your kids will be older, and you'll wish for just one more chaotic day to relive. Soak it in while you can—the mess, the noise, the laughter—because it's all part of the beautiful, messy ride!

If you have thoroughly enjoyed reading this book, please consider leaving a review on the Amazon page. Your vote of confidence allows other curious parents to discover the advice hidden in these pages.

BONUS CONTENT:

Additional Resources

This chapter provides bonus material that you can refer to get more information outside of the book. Here, you will find book recommendations, reputable professional support services, and practical stress management practices that you can add to your self-regulation toolkit.

Must Read Books: Parenting and Personal Growth

You have gained insight into your parenting approach by reading this book. However, we haven't covered everything you need to know about raising children. Below are book recommendations to promote continuous learning and boost your confidence in parenting your children.

The Whole-Brain Child

Authors: Daniel J. Siegel and Tina Payne Bryson

Description: The book explores the science and psychology of healthy brain development by presenting 12 key strategies to nurture your child's mind so they can live a calm, balanced, and meaningful life (Siegel & Payne Bryson, 2016).

How to Stop Losing Your Sh*t with Your Kids

Author: Carla Naumburg

Description: The book takes a compassionate approach to offering evidence-based strategies that help parents regulate intense emotions, preventing unstable moods, meltdowns, and, ultimately, projecting negative emotions onto children (Naumburg, 2020).

Raising Good Humans

Author: Hunter Clarke-Fields

Description: The book combines mindfulness and parenting strategies to help raise compassionate and confident children. Its main goal is to help parents move away from reactive parenting toward conscious parenting (Clarke-Fields, 2020).

Daring Greatly

Author: Brené Brown

Description: The essay explores the power of vulnerability and how this emotion can affect how we see ourselves, relate to each other, and build meaningful relationships with other people. Readers are encouraged to embrace the discomfort of feeling emotionally exposed and express their authentic selves (Brown, 2012).

Parenting from the Inside Out

Authors: Daniel J. Siegel and Mary Hartzell

Description: The book examines how our childhood experiences shape our parenting, using insights from neurobiology and attachment research to offer a step-by-step approach for parents to understand their own life stories better and raise compassionate, resilient children (Siegel & Hartzell, 2014).

Professional and Peer Support Services

Parenting isn't a job that you are expected to manage alone. Apart from reaching out to your close friends and family who can offer emotional support, you can explore professional support services from doctors and therapists or join peer support groups where you become part of a community of parents going through similar stages and challenges. Here are some great resources to consider.

BetterHelp

BetterHelp is a popular mental health platform that can match parents with professional and licensed therapists who provide physical and online counseling. The directory consists of various types of therapy, and results can be filtered by location, availability, and preferences.

Talkspace

Talkspace is an online therapy platform that comes with a downloadable app. Similar to BetterHelp, the platform helps parents find suitable licensed therapists according to their needs and budget. They have also partnered with health insurance providers, meaning you don't have to pay upfront depending on your coverage.

Postpartum Support International (PSI)

Postpartum Support International (PSI) is an organization that raises awareness about the psychological changes women go through during pregnancy and after childbirth. They focus on helping parents with anxiety or postpartum depression get the support they need by providing a helpline, online support groups, and access to educational resources.

Mothers of Preschoolers (MOPS)

Mothers of Preschoolers (MOPS), now simply known as the Mom Community (MomCo), is a global community of Christian women, mothers, and leaders who host local meetup events where members can come together and socialize, seek parenting advice, and build long-lasting friendships.

La Leche League International

La Leche League offers breastfeeding support for new and experienced mothers through local groups, online forums, and resources. It helps mothers with advice, encouragement, and evidence-based information on breastfeeding and infant care.

Parents Helping Parents (PHP)

PHP is a peer-support organization that connects parents dealing with the emotional and practical challenges of raising children with disabilities or special needs. They offer online resources, support groups, and personalized guidance.

The Village

The Village is a community-based platform that connects parents with each other to share resources, advice, and emotional support. It offers a space for parents to find support for both everyday parenting challenges and unique family situations.

Self-Soothing Stress Management Practices

What are your go-to stress management techniques when you are feeling triggered, overwhelmed, or overcome with self-doubt? To add to your existing coping strategies, here are more ways to self-soothe and regain control of your thoughts and emotions during stressful times. Note that many of these practices aren't confined to a specific location, so you can practice them anywhere, and in between or during tasks.

Mindful Breathing

Mindful breathing is the simple practice of paying attention to your breath. Often, in times of stress, your breathing becomes irregular and leads to hyperventilation and stress. Focusing on your breathing can calm your nervous system and deactivate the stress response. Mindful breathing can be done anywhere, anytime. All you need is focus and a few tips to remember, such as:

- Breathe through your nose and out of your mouth.
- Slow your breathing deliberately (it helps to count in your head).
- Make sure that your breath travels to your belly to get as much air into your lungs.
- Whenever you are distracted, shift your focus back to your breathing.

Gratitude Journaling

Gratitude journaling is the practice of writing down what you are grateful for. You can decide whether to write short notes or long reflection pieces about the moments and events that make you stop and appreciate being a parent. What you feel grateful for doesn't need to be something big; everyday small victories count too. To make the most of your journaling practice, follow these tips:

- Dedicate a specific time during the day for journaling (preferably, make it the final task for the day).
- Choose a theme to focus on, such as health, career, parenting, family, or hobbies. This ensures that you cover different aspects of your life.
- After you have written your journal entry, reflect on what you wrote and how far you have come. Recall a time when you were in an unfavorable situation and didn't see life the way you view it now.

- Share your experience with a close friend or family member. Let them know what you're grateful for so that they can celebrate your growth.

Stretching Routine

Stretching is a light form of exercise with physical and mental health benefits, such as increasing serotonin levels, reducing stress, and stabilizing your moods (Adams, 2021). The best part is that stretching is safe for most individuals and doesn't take up too much time. With that said, practicing caution is important to prevent injuries. Here are tips to remember when setting up a stretching routine:

- Decide how often you are going to stretch per week and for how many minutes. Generally, it's recommended to stretch daily but beginners can aim for two to three times per week.
- Warm up before you start stretching to activate your major muscle groups. This can be as simple as marching with your arms swinging for a minute.
- Have a series of light to moderate stretches already planned. Do your research to find stretches that target specific muscle groups. Take note of the suitability of each stretch for your age, body, health status, and flexibility.
- Pay attention to your posture and form during each stretch to prevent injuries. For example, you might need to stand up straight, slightly bend your knee, or move in a certain motion.
- Feeling discomfort while stretching is normal, but it shouldn't be painful. You must stop immediately when the exercise starts to hurt and rest your body. Moreover, practice slow breathing throughout the stretching routine to ease tension and make yourself feel comfortable.

Morning Meditation

There are many different ways that you can start your day to set a positive tone, and one of them is with a morning meditation. In many cultures and religions, meditation is a practice used to reconnect with yourself or the present moment. It gives you a chance to break away from your thoughts and tune into your reality. As a parent, especially when you're running on a busy schedule, meditation can help you focus on what matters most so you don't feel burdened by unnecessary thoughts or tasks. A basic meditation routine goes like this:

- Find a comfortable room or area where you can be alone and meditate.
- Close your eyes and begin breathing slowly.
- It is enough to focus on your breathing, noticing the pace, rhythm, and temperature. However, you can also choose to focus on spontaneous thoughts or emotions that surface—acknowledging them and then letting them go.
- Throughout the meditation, regularly listen to your body to pick up cues about how you are feeling. Notice the physical sensations that arise whenever certain thoughts or emotions come into your mind. Make observations without judging your experiences or getting lost in them.

Setting Daily Intentions

Daily intentions are positive statements that describe how you desire your day to go. Imagine that you had a magical wand and could experience any kind of day you wished. Your intentions are those wishes you make to yourself as a reminder that you can achieve anything you set your mind on. They allow you to shift your mindset toward the outcomes you want instead of those you don't want. Furthermore, you create a motivating goal that you can strive toward. Consider the following tips when you set daily intentions:

- Keep your statements positive and reassuring. Avoid negative language like "can't" or "should not" since this causes you to focus on things you don't want. An example of a positive intention is, "Today, I make a conscious effort to be empathetic toward my children."

- Set intentions that align with your core values to make them feel meaningful. For example, if you value cooperation, you can set intentions that seek better cooperation with your family such as "Today, I welcome support from my partner and children."
- Make your intentions actionable and things that you can achieve by switching your mindset and attitude. The emphasis should be on making changes now and taking different actions throughout the day to improve your experiences. Actionable intentions are also easily measured, so at the end of the day, you can see whether you were able to achieve them or not.

Nature Walks

Nature walks combine mindfulness with physical activity. Being surrounded by nature reduces stress and uplifts your mood, leaving you feeling rejuvenated. Additionally, the peacefulness of nature calms your mind and puts you in a reflective state. Whenever you need a moment to catch your breath or think about decisions, put on your shoes and take a walk outside. Find a scenic route, like walking through a park or road with lined-up trees, and absorb the colors, smells, sounds, and sights around you. Here are other ways to make your nature walks interesting:

- Talk to yourself out loud so you can hear your thoughts.
- Take a walk with your partner or children and use it as a bonding session.
- Take photos of the nature you see on your walk.
- Take a pen and notebook with you so you can journal or write down inspirational ideas that come up during your walk.

Positive Affirmations

Parents don't always give themselves credit for the work they are doing in raising their children and how much they have grown in the process. Positive affirmations are statements that remind you of who you are, what you can accomplish, and the infinite potential trapped inside of you. The science behind positive affirmations is that positive language has the power to pierce into the subconscious mind and change thought patterns. You can positively transform your mindset and behaviors by repeatedly rehearsing positive statements about yourself and your parenting journey. There are countless positive affirmations that you can find online, but here are steps to make your own:

- Use positive and emotive language that makes you believe in yourself. It's essential to speak of yourself like you're a champion, even on days when you don't feel like one. The language you use should reflect who you envision yourself to be and motivate you to become that person.

- Write your affirmations in the present tense, as though the action were happening right now. This suggests to your mind that you are already the person that you desire to be. For example, instead of saying, "I will learn to handle my emotions better," you can say, "I have control over my emotions."

- Create affirmations as a response to your limitations or the challenges you're facing. This allows you to have something positive to say whenever your inner critic brings up your shortcomings. For example, whenever you think, "I'm not like other moms," you can quickly say to yourself, "My uniqueness is what makes me an amazing mom."

Digital Detox

A digital detox is a period of abstinence from technology, usually taken when being online starts contributing to your stress. It involves staying away from your electronic devices or significantly limiting the hours you spend on them (if you cannot completely go offline). Another way to structure your digital detox is to refrain from using specific social media apps or going onto specific websites. Essentially, whatever screen habits that are causing stress can be addressed by distancing yourself from them for a few days or weeks. You get to decide how long the detox lasts and what offline activities you can choose to replace your screen time. Here are more tips to help you:

- Set firmer boundaries around technology, such as the hours you can spend online, the times when you can go online, or the areas in the house where technology is banned.
- Inform your close friends and family about your upcoming digital detox and arrange alternative ways for them to reach out to you.
- Make constructive use of the time during the detox to get some much-needed downtime, explore offline hobbies, or spend quality time with your family.

Scheduled Family Moments

Scheduled family moments bring everyone together and allow you to nurture your relationships. They help you reduce stress by creating opportunities for open communication where you can share your thoughts and feelings. Being around loved ones can also give you a boost of oxytocin, also known as "the bonding chemical," making you feel a greater emotional connection to your family. Consider the following suggestions for scheduled moments you can have with your family:

- Turn your Friday afternoons or evenings into family nights by arranging different games or watching movies together.
- Create fun challenges that allow family members to have friendly competition. For instance, you can host a cook-off, fire-making challenge, dance challenge, or obstacle course race.
- Once or twice a month, tour the city with your family and visit interesting tourist attractions like museums, art galleries, or aquariums. Older children might appreciate trendy places like new pop-up restaurants or going to the mall.
- Maintain a healthy lifestyle by staying active as a family. You can find adventurous sports or activities that are suitable for all ages, such as hiking, riding bikes, swimming, or playing football.

These additional resources show you that help is abundant and available whenever you feel stuck or discouraged on your parenting journey. Some days, you may need the advice of an unbiased third party and other days, you may simply need a 10-minute meditation to ground yourself and regain perspective. Whatever it is, just know that you can overcome those parenting hurdles and emerge stronger and more resilient!

References

Abramson, A. (2021, October 1). *The impact of parental burnout.* American Psychological Association. https://www.apa.org/monitor/2021/10/cover-parental-burnout

Adams, B. (2021, June 23). *The simple act of stretching.* Center for Healthy Aging Colorado State University. https://www.research.colostate.edu/healthyagingcenter/2021/06/23/the-simple-act-of-stretching/

Adriane. (2020, February 22). *How to define and discover your family values.* Raising Kids with Purpose. https://raisingkidswithpurpose.com/defining-family-values/

Amabile, T. M., & Kramer, S. J. (2011, May). *The power of small wins.* Harvard Business Review. https://hbr.org/2011/05/the-power-of-small-wins

American Academy of Pediatrics. (2024, January 23). *How to understand your child's temperament.* Healthy Children. https://www.healthychildren.org/English/ages-stages/gradeschool/Pages/How-to-Understand-Your-Childs-Temperament.aspx

Anonymous. (2020, January 14). *Our family is just the right mix of chaos and love quote.* Quote Pond. https://quotepond.com/family-quotes/

Assertive communication: The DESO framework. (2020, July 24). Related Perspectives. https://www.relatedperspectives.com/post/assertive-communication-the-deso-framework

Atkins, S. (2019). *A quote from Born to Eat.* Goodreads. https://www.goodreads.com/quotes/9058539-there-is-no-such-thing-as-a-perfect-parent-so

Ballard, D. (2023, March 24). *Delegating tasks to our children*. Mom Training. https://www.momtraining.org/blog/delegating-tasks-to-our-children

Bentley, R. (2024, August 1). *How to create a sanctuary at home (2024)*. Architectural Digest. https://www.architecturaldigest.com/reviews/home-improvement/sanctuary-at-home

Brady-Cronin, A. (2023, November 16). *Boundaries not limits - a story of unconditional love*. Anne Brady Cronin. https://annebradycronin.com/boundaries-not-limits-a-story-of-unconditional-love/

Brown, B. (2012). *Daring greatly: How the courage to be vulnerable transforms the way we live, love, parent, and lead*. Penguin Books Ltd.

Brown, B. (2022, March 18). *Fifteen inspiring parenting quotes to live by* (S. Reed, Ed.). Care. https://www.care.com/c/inspirational-parenting-quotes/

Buttery, M. (2022, November 2). *Stigma holds parents back from seeking advice and help. But what can we actually do to de-stigmatise parenting programmes?* Chamber UK. https://chamberuk.com/parenting-programmes/

Caroline. (2014, June 18). *The objective parenting challenge*. Medium; Mum in Progress. https://medium.com/mum-in-progress/the-objective-parenting-challenge-ec0e2b74acab

Children developing independence: What is the right balance? (n.d.). Bright Horizons. https://www.brighthorizons.co.uk/family-zone/family-resources/additional-resources/work-and-young-children/children-independence

Chisholm, A. (2017, February 8). Postpartum depression: The worst kept secret. *Harvard Health Blog*. https://www.health.harvard.edu/blog/postpartum-depression-worst-kept-secret-2017020811008

Clark, S. J., & Woolford, S. J. (2023). Sharing on parenting: Getting advice through social media. In G. L. Freed (Ed.), *Mott Poll*.

Susan B. Meister Child Health Evaluation and Research Center. https://mottpoll.org/reports/sharing-parenting-getting-advice-through-social-media

Clarke-Fields, H. (2020). *Raising good humans: A mindful guide to breaking the cycle of reactive parenting and raising kind, confident kids.* New Harbinger Publications.

Coulson, J. (2013, August 4). *Ten ways to have a positive influence on your children.* Happy Families. https://happyfamilies.com.au/articles/10-ways-to-have-a-positive-influence-on-your-children

Cuzzone, K. (2022, November 14). *How to actually, finally, truly set some boundaries with your family this holiday season.* Wondermind. https://www.wondermind.com/article/setting-boundaries-with-family/

Darcy, A. M. (2022, August 2). *Emotional trigger, or just big emotion?* Harley Therapy. https://harleytherapy.com/blog/posts/emotional-trigger-or-just-big-emotion

Dweck, C. S. (2019). Mindset by Carol S. Dweck. In *PenguinRandomhouse.com.* Penguin Random House. https://www.penguinrandomhouse.com/books/44330/mindset-by-carol-s-dweck-phd/

Edison, T. A. (2024). *Thomas A. Edison quote.* A-Z Quotes. https://www.azquotes.com/quote/518391

Edlynn, E. (2024, March 15). *What is a "good" parent?* Substack.com. https://emilyedlynn.substack.com/p/what-is-a-good-parent

Expectations: what to ignore in the newborn period. (2017, June 30). Your Family's Journey. https://www.yourfamilysjourney.com/knowing-unrealistic-expectations-ignore/

Fisic, J. (2022, April 26). *How to ask for help professionally & politely: A guide with practical examples.* Pumble Blog. https://pumble.com/blog/ask-for-help-professionally/#how-to-ask-for-help-professionally-7-tips-for-requesting-assistance-at-the-workplace

Fox, J. (2021, February 11). *How to celebrate small wins and make greater progress*. Feel More Connected. https://feelmoreconnected.com/how-to-celebrate-small-wins/

Glembocki, V. (2023, February 19). *Six simple ways to be a more present parent*. Parents. https://www.parents.com/parenting/better-parenting/advice/simple-ways-to-be-a-more-present-parent/

Gregston, M. (2010, April 2). *Super hero or not?* Parenting Today's Teens. https://parentingtodaysteens.org/articles/super-hero-super-spoiler/

Hall, J. (2020, July 22). *Four tips for creating a balanced family dynamic*. Complete Family Treatment Services. https://www.completefamilytreatment.com/four-tips-for-creating-a-balanced-family-dynamic/#:~:text=The%20most%20direct%20way%20to

Hall, K. (2014, July 12). Self-validation. *Psychology Today South Africa*. https://www.psychologytoday.com/za/blog/pieces-mind/201407/self-validation

Harvard Health Publishing. (2019). *Six tips for safe stretches* . Harvard Health. https://www.health.harvard.edu/staying-healthy/six-tips-for-safe-stretches

Harvey, B. (2015, December 21). *Positive parenting defined*. Kars4Kids Parenting. https://parenting.kars4kids.org/positive-parenting-defined/

Hinds, S. (2020, July 19). *"It takes a village to raise a child" — african proverb. here's why it's true*. Medium. https://medium.com/@sherlaine.hinds/it-takes-a-village-to-raise-a-child-african-proverb-heres-why-it-s-true-53122b998801

Hodgson, R. (2023, May 16). *The ripple effect of prioritizing your health: How self-care benefits those around you*. LinkedIn. https://www.linkedin.com/pulse/ripple-effect-prioritizing-your-health-how-self-care-benefits-ryan/

Hogg, T., & Blau, M. (2006). *The baby whisperer solves all your problems.* Simon and Schuster. https://www.amazon.com/Baby-Whisperer-Solves-Your-Problems/dp/0743488946

Huelke-Pfleger, L. (2018, November 15). New dads can get the baby blues, too. *Edward-Elmhurst Health.* https://www.eehealth.org/blog/2018/11/paternal-perinatal-depression-and-anxiety/

Huggins, M. (2022, August 12). *Growth mindset: Growth oriented feedback between parent and child.* One with the Water. https://onewiththewater.org/growth-mindset-growth-oriented-feedback-parent-child/

Identity development theory. (2022). Lumen Learning. https://courses.lumenlearning.com/adolescent/chapter/identity-development-theory/

Jafarian, M., & Ananthakrishnan, V. (n.d.). *Understanding adolescence, acting out, and calls for help.* Vera Institute of Justice. https://www.vera.org/when-misbehaving-is-a-crime/what-are-status-offenses

Kanji, S. (2021, February 24). *Finding your passion (your passion).* Youth Are Awesome. https://youthareawesome.com/finding-your-passion-your-passion/

Kostiana, M. (2023, February 22). *Why is it important to know how to delegate as a mother?* Medium. https://mkostiana.medium.com/why-is-it-important-to-know-how-to-delegate-as-a-mother-a5049d205044

Lagioia, V. (2023, April 27). *How to help parents find the right parenting support for them.* Emerging Minds. https://emergingminds.com.au/resources/how-to-help-parents-find-the-right-parenting-support-for-them/

Lamott, A. (n.d.). *A quote by Anne Lamott.* Goodreads. https://www.goodreads.com/quotes/6830146-almost-everything-will-work-again-if-you-unplug-it-for

Matthews, D. (2023, November 14). Growth mindset parenting. *Psychology Today*. https://www.psychologytoday.com/us/blog/going-beyond-intelligence/202311/growth-mindset-parenting

Merriam-Webster. (2019). *Definition of strength*. Merriam-Webster. https://www.merriam-webster.com/dictionary/strength

Mitra, S. (n.d.). *Importance of Encouraging Individuality in Children*. Global Indian School. https://globalindianschool.org/sg/blog-detail/importance-of-encouraging-individuality-in-children

Mosunic, C. (n.d.). The power of setting intentions and how to set mindful ones. *Calm Blog*. https://www.calm.com/blog/setting-intentions

Msingi Afrika Team. (2022, March 31). *The mini-me syndrome*. Msingi Afrika Magazine. https://www.msingiafrikamagazine.com/2022/04/the-mini-me-syndrome/

Nasamran, A. (2021, February 15). Why do children act out and what to do about it. *Atlas Psychology*. https://www.atlaspsychologycollective.com/blog/why-do-children-act-out

Naumburg, C. (2020). How to stop losing your sh*t with your kids: A practical guide to becoming a calmer, happier parent. In *Amazon.com*. Audible Studios. https://www.amazon.com/How-Stop-Losing-Your-Kids/dp/B083JJCF1Y/ref=sr_1_1?dib=eyJ2IjoiMSJ9.od1zDudS9tzEeuNtXStphl_p-KVsUM81WofjhHKpIl3GjHj071QN20LucGBJIEps.CUfEOyOUu-7PaOUcFe9vV-tcRHGcpuTuNH0LfrdZht0&dib_tag=se&keywords=How+to+Stop+Losing+Your+Sh

Navigating the emotional landscape of new parenthood. (2024, February 10). Lyndhurst Gynecologic Associates. https://www.lyndhurstgyn.com/emotional-landscape-of-new-parenthood/

Neff, K. (2024). *What is self-compassion?* Self-Compassion. https://self-compassion.org/what-is-self-compassion/

Nelson, C. (2023, May 10). *The 4 types of parenting styles: What style is right for you?* Mayo Clinic Press. https://mcpress.mayoclinic.org/parenting/what-parenting-style-is-right-for-you/

Normal functioning family. (2015, November 21). Healthy Children. https://www.healthychildren.org/English/family-life/family-dynamics/Pages/Normal-Family-Functioning.aspx

Obama, M. (2015). *Michelle Obama quote*. A-Z Quotes. https://www.azquotes.com/quote/1294014

Ogunsina, A. (2023, March 20). *The impact of social media on modern parenting: The good, the bad, the ugly*. LinkedIn. https://www.linkedin.com/pulse/impact-social-media-modern-parenting-good-bad-ugly-adewale-ogunsina/

Parenting and social media use: The modern influence. (2024, April 21). Riaz Counseling. https://riazcounseling.com/parenting-and-social-media-use-the-modern-influence/

Parents, are we overdoing the selflessness? (2023). Aim Montessori Teacher Training. https://aimmontessoriteachertraining.org/parents-are-we-overdoing-the-selflessness/

Porrey, M. (2023, October 12). *What is enmeshment, and how do you set boundaries?* Verywell Health. https://www.verywellhealth.com/enmeshment-healing-steps-5223635

Rogers, F. (2021, June 16). What is the inside story to the outside behavior? Our children's emotions behind the behavior (M. Waldman, Ed.). *My Feel Links*. https://myfeellinks.com/blogs/news/what-is-the-inside-story-to-the-outside-behavior-our-childrens-emotions-behind-the-behavior

Rooney, E. A. (2023, April 7). *Mom guilt - we all feel it*. LinkedIn. https://www.linkedin.com/pulse/mom-guilt-we-all-feel-erica-anderson-rooney/

Roosevelt, E. (2024, February 29). Prioritizing yourself quotes: 101 quotes that will inspire you (C. Rooney, Ed.). *The Blogging Lifestyle*. https://theblogginglifestyle.com/prioritizing-yourself-quotes/

Scheib, E. (2018, April 13). *Why alone time is crucial for introverted moms (and how to stop guilt)*. Introvert Dear. https://introvertdear.com/news/introverted-moms-guilty-alone-time/

Self care and resilience. (2024). University of Cumbria. https://my.cumbria.ac.uk/Student-Life/Health-and-Wellbeing/My-Mental-Health--Wellbeing-Hub/Self-Care-and-Resilience/

Siegel, D. J., & Hartzell, M. (2014). *Parenting from the inside out : how a deeper self-understanding can help you raise children who thrive*. Jeremy P. Tarcher.

Siegel, D. J., & Payne Bryson, T. (2016). *The whole-brain child : 12 revolutionary strategies to nurture your child's developing mind*. Langara College.

Siegel, S. (2021, September 28). Four expectations of new mothers that are downright wrong! *Unique Footprints*. https://www.uniquefootprints.com/blog/expectations

Support for parents: why it's important and where to get it. (2023, August 30). Raising Children Network. https://raisingchildren.net.au/grown-ups/services-support/about-services-support/support-for-parents-why-its-important

Time management tips for busy parents. (2024). *Bright Horizons*. https://www.brighthorizons.co.uk/family-zone/family-resources/blog/2022/03/time-management-tips-for-busy-parents

Top tips to encourage independence in toddlers. (2020, September 8). Only about Children. https://www.oac.edu.au/news-views/top-tips-to-encourage-independence-in-toddlers/

Travers, M. (2024, August 28). Two signs of an "emotionally intelligent parent," from A psychologist. *Forbes.* https://www.forbes.com/sites/traversmark/2024/08/27/2-signs-of-an-emotionally-intelligent-parent-from-a-psychologist/

Unknown. (2024). *Being A parent can be tough quote.* Mind Family. https://mind.family/quotes/being-a-parent-can-be-tough/

Image References

Ahuja, A. (2021). A girl showing her homework to her parents [Image]. In *Pexels.* https://www.pexels.com/photo/a-girl-showing-her-homework-to-her-parents-8055086/

Bauso, E. (2019). Family of four walking at the street [Image]. In *Pexels.* https://www.pexels.com/photo/family-of-four-walking-at-the-street-2253879/

Bauso, E. (2020). Woman holding mans hand [Image]. In *Pexels.* https://www.pexels.com/photo/woman-holding-man-s-hand-3585811/

Bolovtsova, K. (2020). A mother spending time with her children [Image]. In *Pexels.* https://www.pexels.com/photo/a-mother-spending-time-with-her-children-4866894/

Burton, K. (2021). Desperate screaming young boy [Image]. In *Pexels.* https://www.pexels.com/photo/desperate-screaming-young-boy-6624327/

Chung, Z. (2020). Ethnic funny girl eating with mother in backyard [Image]. In *Pexels.* https://www.pexels.com/photo/ethnic-funny-girl-eating-with-mother-in-backyard-5528983/

Cottonbro Studio. (2020). A woman reading a book [Image]. In *Pexels*. https://www.pexels.com/photo/a-woman-reading-a-book-5485799/

Green, A. (2020). Middle aged female knitting with needles [Image]. In *Pexels*. https://www.pexels.com/photo/relaxed-middle-aged-female-knitting-with-needles-5691915/

Kaboompics, K. (2020). Close-up shot of a person doing her homework [Image]. In *Pexels*. https://www.pexels.com/photo/close-up-shot-of-a-person-doing-her-homework-5311619/

Kampus Production. (2021). A family sitting on cushions on the floor while meditating together [Image]. In *Pexels*. https://www.pexels.com/photo/a-family-sitting-on-cushions-on-the-floor-while-meditating-together-7417130/

Krukau, Y. (2020). A mother using laptop with her son [Image]. In *Pexels*. https://www.pexels.com/photo/a-mother-using-laptop-with-her-son-4458320/

www.ingramcontent.com/pod-product-compliance
Lightning Source LLC
Chambersburg PA
CBHW040233110526
44582CB00002B/45